Praise for *Dare t*

Dare to Be the Change chronicles a journey of overcoming adversity and building strong professional relationships to become a success in a rapidly evolving corporate landscape. The power of addressing complex workplace issues head-on, revising one's strategy, and focusing on goals shines through this compelling story of perseverance and courage. This book is an excellent read for anyone wanting inspiration for personal and professional growth.
—Kimberly J. Fontenot, CFP, Financial Advisor

In *Dare to Be the Change*, Annella Metoyer offers a candid, unique perspective on how the unavoidable changes in life can refine a person's character or destroy it. Her father's sage question during her childhood difficulties, "If you don't do it, who will?" formed an early fortification and guide throughout her life. Her encouraging story is one of resilience and determination. Her personal struggle to find meaning in life after an involuntary end to her amazing forty-year career as a banking executive will resonate with many readers and leaders! Readers will find solace in knowing they are not alone and discover new options worth pursuing if, in fact, they "dare to be the change."
—Eddie Turner, Leadership Expert,
Executive Coach and Facilitator,
Eddie Turner, LLC

Dare to Be the Change is a book of courage, hope, and decisive change, filled with stories that enlighten the reader's heart with new perspective and clarity. In this book, author Annella Metoyer courageously shares the details of her personal and professional challenges to offer hope for readers through her family's dedication to positive change and her accomplishments. I have known Annella as a performance improvement coach who uses personality types to create strategic results for organizations. I am wowed by Annella's surefootedness, inspirational influence, and ability to use her keen observations to create certainty in chaotic environments. This book is for anyone who holds hope deep within their heart and wishes to transform their adversities into accomplishments.

—Gagan Sarkaria, High-Achievement Wellness & Business Coach | www.UnfoldYourSuccess.com

This is a must read for anyone in business today. Annella writes with such authenticity and is a living testament how one person can truly change the world, through southern graciousness. She is the consummate professional, collaborator, and the most excellent example of being a leader of change.

—Kim Nugent, Ed. D., Trainer, Speaker, and Author of *Did I Say Never?*

This deeply personal account of life from rural Louisiana to the banking board room is both inspirational and triumphant. In *Dare to be the Change*, Annella shares personal and professional experiences in vivid detail to reveal how we can overcome challenging situations and make a significant difference in the lives of others.

—Janet Melancon, Executive Coach & HR Consultant, Janet Melancon Associates

The story allowed me to peer inside Annella's heart and mind as she traversed her career path. It was a complete joy and kept me wondering what was next for her. I felt satisfaction as she made each step a life lesson to be shared with readers.

—Karen Love, Director, Practice Growth, PKF of Texas, P.C. - CPAs and Professional Advisors

Annella Metoyer very candidly takes us on a personal journey of challenge, perseverance, and ultimately self-triumph. Her book, *Dare to Be the Change*, is a primer to others seeking a career in the corporate world, with all the warts and all. Here is a woman who went all in, got burned, but came out happy in the end. Salud!

—Minerva Perez, Journalist and Author of *I Gotta Story: My 30 Years in TV News*

This is a must read for anyone that has an interest in professional and personal growth. This vulnerable and risk-taking story highlights a journey filled with overcoming challenges and creating opportunities. The story of race relations, diversity and holding steadfast to the principle that people and relationships matter above all else, remains relevant today. It also reminds us that determination and optimism are necessary pillars for a healthy life.

—Michael T. Pugh, President & Chief Executive Officer, Carver Federal Savings Bank

Dare to Be the Change

by Annella Metoyer

Dedication

This book is dedicated to my father, Martel John Goodly, for being the change and to all the great people who continue to open doors for others.

There is no illusion greater than fear.

—Lao Tzu

Table of Contents

Preface

My over forty years in the corporate world gave me the opportunity to have many firsts. First in positions not held by a female or a person of color. Thus, I faced many adversities, Michelle Obama once said, "Your experience facing and overcoming adversity is actually one of your biggest advantages." I was determined to turn these challenges into learnings for myself. By sharing my story, I now allow others to learn from these challenges as well.

The journey of this book started many years ago. Throughout my career, I shared my experiences to capture individuals' imaginations, broaden their knowledge, and help them see another point of view. Sometimes I saw a new birth in them, reducing hatred associated with racism. Telling your story can educate others and open a new bridge of understanding. The strong urge to tell my story in book form expressed itself in my dreams and conversations with others. For years, I started writing this book but could not finish.

In October 2016, one dream started to become a reality. I woke up one morning and shared with my husband that I would be attending a retreat. When he asked which one, I told him I was not sure, yet I knew I would be attending a retreat in the new year.

In January 2017, a friend of mine, Dr. Kim Nugent, shared with me that she had written a book in a weekend. My first thought was, *In a weekend? Impossible*. Writing a book takes months, sometimes years. Kim continued to tell me the story of her interaction at a Tom Bird retreat. The more she shared, the more I listened. Soon afterward, she requested I attend a retreat with her in Sedona,

Arizona. Without hesitation, I said yes. When I shared Kim's story and invitation with my husband, he was surprised I would be attending a book-writing retreat. Little did I know the retreat would be a life-changing experience.

The prep work started with Tom Bird's *Write to Heal* book. The healing process in his book helped make way for my writing process. When I arrived in Sedona, many surprises lay ahead. The retreat gave attendees the opportunity to open our hearts and forgive. Within two days, not only had I written a book, I had also started a new chapter in my journey.

As you read, you may discover you and I have faced some of the same challenges, or you may expand your awareness of challenges unfamiliar to you. I take you on my journey with the hope you will walk away with new understanding and rejoice in the strength to make this world a better place.

Acknowledgments

I want to thank Dr. Kim Nugent for supporting me, not only through my transition from the corporate world but also for the gift of introducing me to Tom Bird and making the book a reality. I would also like to thank Tom Bird for being supportive throughout the process of writing, revising, and revising again. Additionally, I would like to thank Denise Cassino and Tori Yabo for your many hours of support and expertise.

Throughout my career, I had the pleasure of working with many amazing people, a few made a difference in my life and many other lives. They supported many individuals when others did not—in other words, they were the voice in the room. Thank you to J. W. Laughlin, Ellen Johnson, Pat Plaia, Lynn Pike, Ricky Otey, Kyle Waters, James Jackson, Steve Hale, Verna Rutherford, Michael Pugh, and Raymond Pereira for opening the doors for so many other deserving individuals.

Thank you to my best friends, Russell Guilbeau and Denise LeBlanc. You were always there when no one else understood. Your support has meant the world to me.

Finally, thank you to my family. My amazing husband, thank you for your love and support even when it was hard. You always said, "Just ride the wave." It has been an amazing ride and continues to be amazing today. Thank you to my mom, Haddie; my dad, Martel; my sisters, Louella, Mary Ella, and Clarice; my son, Jason; and my grandson, Christopher. You have always been my foundation, and we are blessed to be family.

Chapter 1

What Color Am I?

I grew up in a small town in Louisiana with a population of fewer than 5,000 residents. The community has a strong sports commitment, what you might call the "Friday night lights" atmosphere. Residents are either consumed with sports or involved in a local church—that's it. Everyone knows everything about everyone, or if not, believe me, they can be very creative.

Our family home was located in the country about five miles out of town, and our closest neighbor lived approximately a half-mile down the road. On the family farm, we raised cows, pigs, sheep, and chickens. We also grew corn, field peas, and cotton. I can still smell the cotton aroma that permeated my parent's clothes after a long day in the fields. Eventually, the cotton crop became soybeans and rice. I was the eldest of four children, so working on the farm was a norm.

My favorite pastime was walking in the nearby woods attached to our property. I loved the smell of pine and the whistle of the breeze through the branches. The wildflowers always made the woody path a magical place. I spent many days walking this path, thinking about what I would one day do with my life. I knew farm life was not in my future. As a small child, I did not like going into the chicken coop to gather eggs. The rooster always stood guard of his domain, reminding me he was in charge. I also remember the smell of the chicken coop—not the most pleasant smell. I guess the smell is what helped me decide that farm life was not for me.

My parents grew up in small farming communities located approximately twenty-five miles from each other.

They both came from hard-working homes. When they married, the tradition of hard work continued throughout their lives. I remember Mom's garden, which supplied fresh vegetables for the family. She would spend hours canning both fruits and vegetables for the winter months. My mother was a self-trained seamstress, and to bring in extra cash, she sewed clothes for the neighbors in the community. To make ends meet, Dad always had three or four jobs. Whether it was working in the rice fields or working at the local wood plant, he worked long hours to provide for the family. He was a military man who served his country during the Korean War. The training in the armed services taught him proficient work methods, and he shared these methods in teaching us how to work.

Every Saturday morning, my sister and I would mop and wax the floors of our house. The paste wax was orange and had an aroma similar to gasoline. We would use an old cloth, and on our knees, carefully spread the orange paste. After the wax dried, to create the perfect shine we would take an old towel and push and pull each other across the floor. Our speed on the slick floors had us laughing for hours.

After we finished cutting grass, washing clothes, and cooking food, Mom would turn on the record player and play zydeco music. The bluesy accordion instrument brings a sound that beckons you to tap your foot. We would dance until we were out of breath. Mom's greatest love was the music, and she lived for the Saturday dance day. After the many dance lessons from Mom, all the girls learned their own version of the zydeco shuffle.

My parents' first language was Creole French; English was their second language. They spoke Creole French most of the time however their conversations with us were in English. Their parents had trained them to speak Creole French at home and English in public. I only

2

learned to speak a few words in Creole French though I understood many conversations.

While I have many great childhood memories, I do not have great memories of my school days. Because I was neither dark-skinned nor white, but somewhere in-between, I experienced bullying from both black and white children.

When I started elementary school, I was at the "colored" school. Here, I did not fit in because my skin was a lighter shade. I was fortunate I had cousins who attended the school with me because I had someone to turn to if needed. In the second grade, the kids started to drift away from me.

One day I decided to pay the other kids one dime per day or buy them candy from the school cantina to play with me. I did this for a long time until my parents noticed the small piggy bank of dimes was drying up. The evening my father found out was not the best night of my life. I stopped giving out dimes immediately and slowly started losing friends again.

In 1965, integration of schools took place in our small-town school district. My father was always seeking a better life for his children, so he decided that his two school-age girls would transfer to the better-funded "white" school. I was in the fifth grade, and my little sister was in the second grade. I was excited about leaving the kids who would not play with me, who picked on me daily for not being dark enough. I hoped the new school would give me an opportunity to be seen as a person and not as the color of my skin.

My new challenge began the first day at my new school. I remember my mother and the principal walking me to meet my new teacher. I stood at the door looking into the classroom. My new classroom was bright with sunshine beaming through the windows. Everything on

3

the teacher's desk was neat and orderly. The walls were painted white, and the blackboards were clean. I gazed at the bulletin board displaying a variety of colorful posters, many more than my previous school that had only a few posters. I gaped, thinking to myself that this new school had money because everything looked brand new.

Within minutes, I watched my mother leave with the principal. Butterflies filled my stomach as my new teacher and I walked toward her desk in the front of the room. As I stood at the front of the room, the teacher introduced me as the new student. The students were staring at me, and no one said a word. The teacher then directed me to my new desk, which was located in the back of the classroom.

As I started what seemed like a long journey to my new desk, one of my new classmates yelled out, "Well, we did not get a black one; instead they sent us a pink nigga." The room filled with laughter. I wanted to turn around and run, but where would I go? The school was a foreign land to me; I knew only this classroom. I continued to walk toward my desk, hoping no one would touch me or trip me along the way. I started thinking that being called "whitey" at my previous school was not so bad in comparison to this nightmare. *Why are my parents doing this to me?* I thought. Trading one hell for another was not my dream of a better opportunity. I finally got to my desk. Everyone was turned around in their seats staring at me. *Am I that ugly?* The teacher looked like she had seen a ghost, for she was extremely pale. She did not know what to do with me. The class was noisy, and the teacher was trying her best to control the class of fifth graders but struggled throughout the day.

The name-calling continued at recess, lunch, and other school activities. Imagine being ten years old, standing in the playground where *everyone* is staring, pointing, and calling you names. How would I overcome this challenge and make new friends? I felt all alone in a very different world. I became increasingly quiet and withdrawn. I tried to appear strong, but deep inside, this hurt. Why was I so different?

To make matters even more unbelievable, we did not ride the new school bus. Instead, we rode the bus from the "colored" school. The "colored" bus was not allowed to drive into the "white" school ground, so we were dropped off a few blocks away to walk the remaining distance. The extra few blocks of walking did not concern us, mainly because we did not know any better. It took my father's lobbying the school board to get the school bus to be able to drop us in front of the school, and an even longer time to get the school board to agree to let us ride the "white" school bus.

Once the school board approved us to ride the "white" bus, we unfortunately dealt with more than we envisioned. My sister and I were assigned a seat in the back of the bus. There was no rebuttal from us about sitting in the back of the bus, except being near the school bully. His joy was sitting with us in our assigned seat and making us move over to the right of the seat until my sister was sitting on my lap. Despite being white herself, the school bus driver was scared to death of the bully, and her attempts to stop him from harassing us did not work. The bullying went on for weeks, until one day, I could not take the bullying anymore. That evening I shared the incident with my father, who again had to lobby the school board, this time to get us moved to the front of the bus.

Years later, I heard the bully beat the bus driver until she was black and blue, yet received only a suspension from school. Thank goodness we had a father who was not afraid to speak up—otherwise, sooner or later, we probably would have been beaten like the bus driver.

Things got better the following two years because more students transferred from the "colored" school. Then, the "colored" school closed. While it was awesome to see friends and cousins, it was sad to see the separation of the students in the new school. The administration did not make an effort to bring students together. It was the unspoken belief that blacks and whites did not mix. We were in the classroom together but separated at lunch, recess, and other activities. This culture continued for the remainder of my elementary, junior high, and high-school years.

One bright spot was my new sixth-grade teacher, Mrs. Murphy. Mrs. Murphy was a young teacher with a beautiful smile of perfect white teeth. My first day in her class, she walked up to my desk and talked to me. I remember my heart fluttering because she was paying attention to me. She was talking to me, smiling. Mrs. Murphy asked a lot of questions about the previous year's studies. I did not know why she was asking, but today I assume she was assessing what I would need in her class. Throughout my first day, she walked over to my desk several times to make sure I understood the subject matter or new assignment. I could not wait to go home to tell Mom about my new teacher.

Every day after the first day, it was the same: she would smile and spend time talking to me. One day, she asked if I would like to come over to her house to bake cupcakes for the class party. *Me?* I told her I would check with my parents and let her know the next day. My mother agreed to let me go over for a couple of hours. I was so excited to have the experience of going to a teacher's home.

When we arrived at her home, it was huge and beautifully decorated. The babysitter of her baby boy talked to her for a few minutes before heading out. Mrs. Murphy's baby was adorable; he smiled just like his mom. While Mrs. Murphy got the baking items together, I played with the baby. As we stirred the cake batter, we talked about school and other matters. It seemed like just fifteen minutes before it was already time to go. I had other opportunities to visit Mrs. Murphy's home during the year and will always be thankful for how she impacted my life. As a child, her kindness opened the door for me to feel included—she was a voice in the room.

I was twelve years old when Dr. Martin Luther King was assassinated. When my school heard the news, all the black kids were moved to the library and held there until our parents came to pick us up, or the bus was ready to take us home. I felt confused about being moved to the library. *A great person has been assassinated, but we are separated because we are "black?"* As a young child, I did not understand that fear drove the school leaders to do this. Fear of the unknown drives individuals to have a quick reaction versus thinking through a situation. Watching everyone's reaction felt like someone was squeezing my inner self, and oh, how my heart and head hurt. As I sat waiting for my name to be called, I decided I needed to do something one day to change how people reacted to our race.

The next day was not any better. It was like having a disease that everyone was afraid to get near. You could feel the fear from both the students and the faculty. There were no conversations about what had taken place, only the sound of students going to and from one classroom to the next. Time did not ease the tension, and there were numerous student fights and parents picketing the school. For a small town, the voices of the people were determined to see change.

One day, one of my cousins got into a fight with a classmate. It was a morning recess, everyone was standing around, and some kids yelled, "Fight!" My cousin's popularity in sports caused girls from every race to admire him. But some Caucasian boys did not approve of the girls' admiration. As the students ran toward the middle of the school playground, I heard someone say that my cousin was in the fight and that there was a knife. I started crying because I was afraid my cousin would die in the fight. Luckily, there was no knife—only a few black eyes and bruises.

At my new school, these were some defining moments in which I was again viewed differently because of the color of my skin—this time, for being darker.

Chapter 2

A Wise Neighbor

Our neighbor, Ms. O'Connor, holds a special place in my heart because she did not judge people by the color of their skin. She was of Irish descent but accepted my family as part of her family. She was not afraid of anything. One day I saw a water moccasin that was approximately five feet in length basking in the sun. With ease, she exterminated the snake with one strike using a garden hoe. She was also aware of the important role snakes played in nature. For example, she always smiled when she saw a king snake, reminding me that they got rid of rodents.

In her own way, Ms. O'Connor was a beautiful woman. She never wore makeup, perfume, or jewelry. Instead, she wore a long cotton dress, an apron, a knit cap, rubber boots, and gloves. She took pride in everything she owned; I knew this from the stories she shared about each item. She would chew tobacco frequently and would spit the tobacco juice in her prized gold spittoon. A widower, she lived alone in a small house overflowing with furniture and memories from her past. Dishes, glasses, bowls, and other goods were stacked on tables, on top of the refrigerator, and on top of the china cabinets. As you carefully walked through the maze, trying hard not to break anything, you could imagine the plates, silverware, and glasses at her family dinner.

On the Saturdays I did not have a lot of chores at home, I would spend the morning helping Ms. O'Connor with her chores. The smell of strong morning coffee was brewing in the silver coffee pot on the stove. I loved the smell but would not join her in drinking the bitter beverage. Instead, I would have a piece of pie or cake and maybe some hot black tea. We always sat at the table that butted up to the kitchen window. As a ten-year-old, I had a lot of energy, so I struggled to sit in one place for a long time. She must have known this because she would say, "Let's go pick the eggs," or "Walk with me to the garden."

I was always amazed by how she would gently slide her hand under each hen and remove the eggs. It seemed like the hens were waiting for her to arrive. As she would remove the eggs, they would jump out of their nest and stand there waiting for their morning breakfast of corn. I would watch them peck into the ground looking for treasures. Their chirping sound was like a band playing a song. I would imagine them talking to each other about the great meal they were having or about us standing there watching them. Their conversations would settle down once they had eaten their fill. Then Ms. O'Connor would open the gate, and the hens would slowly set out for an adventure.

Ms. O'Connor's greatest love was working in her garden. The rows and rows of vegetables lined up perfectly. There were tomatoes large and small, followed by mustard and collard greens, butter beans, green onions, okra, cucumbers, beets and anything else that would grow in the sandy soil. For years, this was Ms. O'Connor's way of making a few dollars to pay the bills. I spent many Saturdays with Ms. O'Connor, helping her with the daily chores. She was always educating me on the importance of hard work, and her work ethic mirrored my parents' work habits. She took the time to teach me how to bake pies, from a coconut pie to an authentic southern pecan pie. The pecan pie mixture of brown sugar, pecans, and Karo syrup still brings back wonderful memories. Today, I continue that tradition by teaching young family members the same baking techniques I learned from her.

My favorite conversations were sharing with Ms. O'Connor what was happening at school. She was my audience, with no heckling from the crowd. She just let me talk and talk about anything and everything. My main topic was the bullying at school. She never judged me for what I was saying—only listened. I would tell her that I was confused about how others treated me. Her advice was always to listen, be open, keep quiet, and walk away from conflicts. She reminded me that "if you cannot say anything nice, do not say anything." She always pointed out what Walter Cronkite reported on the nightly news, so I believe she was concerned that if I spoke up, it might be harmful to me. It took me many years to learn when it was the right time to speak up.

Recently, I visited her grave with my mother and father for the first time since her death. I wanted to thank her for giving me many gifts. I also wanted to assure her that I was sharing my learnings with others. As I stood there in front of her grave with flowers in hand, I felt an enormous sadness come over me. For someone who spent hours planting flowers for others, her grave was without flowers. As I placed the flowers in the vase, I promised myself I would always return with flowers in hand.

Sometimes God puts a person like Ms. O'Connor in our lives to remind us that there are fearlessly loving people in the world. She was a great support to our family at a time when many were not open to people of color.

Chapter 3

If You Don't, Who Will?

In 1972, the end of my junior year in high school, the young, cheerful, energetic school activity director, Ms. Susan, decided she would integrate the cheerleader squad—by asking me to try-out. I shared with her that I did not know how to do a cartwheel or any of the cheers the other girls knew. However, she would not hear of it; she was determined that I would be part of the tryouts. She explained to me what being "first" meant and described some of the challenges I would face being a cheerleader.

I knew my parents would not be happy with the short-skirted uniform. On the other hand, I knew they would be proud that I would be changing the face of the cheerleader squad, a first for the school. My father had a great saying when a change was necessary: "If you don't do it, who will?" He told this to many who sought his advice. I knew change was necessary to move the school forward, so I signed up for tryouts and started the prep work to compete.

The day of tryouts, I watched each white competitor do her routine. I stood there frightened, because my routine was, at best, mediocre. When the judge called my name, I ran out to the middle of the gym. I looked up at the crowd in the stands, and the students were pointing and laughing. I did not understand what they were saying, but it made me nervous. I quickly did my cheer and ended it with a small jump. The crowd was clapping softly, but I was happy that someone in the audience was clapping. I walked back to the end of the competitor line and thought, *No way will I qualify.* Still Ms. Susan was persistent in changing the face of the squad. I am sure she had something to do with the final roster.

When the names of the selected were called, I never heard my name. One of the senior cheerleaders came over and pulled me back onto the floor. I looked around the gym, and everyone was clapping, shouting, and smiling. Then one of the senior cheerleaders started a new cheer, and we had to follow along. I know I must have looked unprepared because, since my family didn't attend many sports activities, I did not know the cheer. I did my best to follow her, but I was embarrassed that I was now a cheerleader and did not know the steps. I am not sure how I made it through that day. I walked around numb, as students came up to me to congratulate me. I was not qualified to be a cheerleader. After being so often excluded because of the color of my skin, it felt odd to be included for the same reason.

Summer came quickly, and it was time to attend cheerleader camp at a nearby college campus. Summer cheerleader camp was the first time I was away from home without my parents. I was excited and a bit scared, but I knew I would have the opportunity to learn the cheers and meet some new friends. When we arrived at the college campus, there were girls, girls, and more girls everywhere. We settled into our rooms and got ready to start the learning process. It was a hot summer, but we did not notice the heat because of the excitement in the air.

Cheerleader camp included a competition between different schools from around the state in various categories. The evening before the first competition, I asked the head cheerleader if we would be practicing our routine. She said I should not worry about practicing and just to follow the lead of the team during the performance. However, I knew they were practicing because I had overheard them talking about it. The next day, I was falling short and struggled to keep up. I knew I would have to work harder to succeed. How do you change the thought process to be included? When the camp was over, I remember going home exhausted from trying to fit in. I slept the entire day and night and was having nightmares of what my senior year would be like as a cheerleader.

Unfortunately, reality was exactly like my dreams. I was not allowed to go to the other cheerleaders' homes to make posters or practice with the team. The families were still struggling to accept a black cheerleader being on the squad. Yes, we went to church together and shopped at the same grocery store, but I was not allowed in their homes. My option was to make a poster alone at home and bring it to the sports event. I wanted to be included, I wanted to do my part, and I wanted to make a difference. How do you make a difference when you are not allowed to be part of the change?

I did make a difference; I was the first cheerleader who was a person of color, thanks to Ms. Susan. Me facing my challenges was an advantage for the many cheerleaders of color who followed. The commitment I had made years earlier in my elementary school library—to be the change—was starting to become a reality.

Chapter 4

Hot Biscuits and Butter

During my senior year of high school, I struggled with what I should do after graduation. My grades were not stellar, so a scholarship was not in the cards, and my parents could not afford to pay for college. Should I join the armed forces, get a job, or just leave home and "find myself"? When I discussed the military with my father, he would not hear of it. I assumed he did not want his daughter to follow in his footsteps. He had previously served as a foot soldier in the Korean War. Also, he grew up in the generation that believed women stayed home, had children, and took care of the family.

About three months before graduation, I decided to find a job and go to college part-time. However, God has a way of opening other doors when you least expect it because, one month before graduation, my father received a call from the president of our local bank. My father had been a customer of the bank for years and knew the president through their many business transactions. In the telephone conversation, the president shared he had an interest in hiring me. The bank had been under pressure to hire minorities, and somehow, the president had chosen me to be the first minority to obtain a job there.

When my father discussed the opportunity with me, I was both excited about the prospect of a new job, but also scared. I was excited because it answered my question of what to do with my life but scared because I knew I would be the first minority working in the bank in our small community. I felt like the weight of the world was on my shoulders because I knew acceptance from the

17

community would not be unanimous. A person of color would be a first for many customers, and change is always difficult.

The day of the meeting, I wore a new dress my mother had sewn. The president talked to my father and me about how he would personally ensure my success. He also listed some expectations of the job. It was a foggy conversation because my father and the president did most of the talking, but the meeting went well. He thanked my father for bringing me in and requested I start right after graduation.

To this day, I often wonder why the president selected me. Was it because of my mother's and father's excellent reputations of hard work? Was it because I stepped out and took the risk of being the first minority cheerleader? Or was it my light skin color? Or maybe, it was my experience working in the school's principal office during my senior year?

The following weekend, my father shared the news with his father, my grandfather and hero. Despite having just an elementary-school education, he was the smartest person I had ever met. He took every challenge in his life and turned it into an advantage. I never heard him say a negative word about anyone. I remember him meeting one of my uncle's girlfriends. Everyone had raised an eyebrow at the young lady, but not my grandfather. He said, "She was really nice and was wearing a pretty dress." As a child, hearing him speak positively gave me a foundation to always look at the bright side of things.

When my father finished describing his meeting with the bank president, my grandfather looked at me and said, "This is a BIG job!" His smile on his face showed me how important this was. I felt butterflies in my stomach. I kept telling myself, *You cannot fail!* That's why Ben Franklin's quote, "By failing to prepare, you are preparing to fail" is my favorite quote. I was going to prepare myself for this new job and make my grandfather proud.

The morning of my first day of work, I woke up early to dress in a new homemade suit. Not sure what to expect, I was both nervous and excited. I arrived early and was let in through the side door by the president. The president and I walked together to his office where Ms. Bella was waiting for me. Ms. Bella worked in the loan department, but since she had knowledge of the various departments throughout the bank, she was my unofficial mentor. The president introduced me to her and reviewed the expectations of the job. I immediately took a liking to Ms. Bella. She had the most contagious smile. I soon learned that the customers loved her as well. Some customers would wait more than an hour just to have their check cashed by Ms. Bella.

When we finished meeting with the president, Ms. Bella gave me a tour of my new workplace. As we toured, she continued to assure me she would help me learn the process of banking. She kept her word—she not only trained me in my new position but also mentored me in how to interact with customers and employees. She and I had long conversations before and after work about the "banking way" of doing things. She was not afraid to coach me when things did not go well. She also knew this was a big change for banking. Looking back, I honestly felt she wanted me to succeed. I was just as determined to be successful, so I took lots of notes and asked a lot of questions.

My first job was stamping the addresses of customers on envelopes, enabling us to mail the statement and checks at the end of the month. I did this eight hours a day, five days a week. I also filed checks in the many drawers of account numbers. It wasn't the most exciting work, but I was happy to have a job.

Soon I found myself making a few "cultural" adjustments. For example, I used to wear many suits and dresses my mother proudly took the time to sew for me. The best suit she sewed was one with colorful stripes—yellow, blue, red, green, purple—a rainbow of colors. When I arrived to work one day with the suit on, the president met me at the door and requested I go home to change into a more conservative piece of clothing. He said, "While your suit looks nice, it's just not appropriate for the banking environment." I quickly went home and changed into a navy-blue banking suit. Thank goodness the president was looking out for me because I can only imagine what customers would have thought.

My next challenge did not take long to arrive. At the end of a work day, I was in the kitchen getting some water to drink, and the assistant to the president came up to me and spoke in a low voice.

"So are you going to give me what you owe me? I am the reason you have this job."

Being naïve, and only seventeen years old, I was mortified someone was saying this to me. I looked at him and said, "I do not know what you mean."

He repeated the request with a big smile.

I said, "I am not like that!" and ran out of the kitchen. I quickly found my purse, got in my car and drove home.

When I arrived home, I told my mother. My mother decided that we should go back immediately to the bank to talk to the president. I'm sure she was horrified someone had made a pass at her young daughter.

The president was working alone in his office and seemed surprised when we arrived. He requested we have a seat in the two chairs in front of his desk. He took the time to listen to my story but showed no emotions. The president assured my mother and me that he would take care of the situation and that this would not happen again. We stood up, my mother thanked him for his time, and we walked back to my car. Mom and I did not say a lot as we drove home, but I could see she was upset.

To his word, no additional incidents happened. The next day, the assistant avoided me at all costs, and I gladly reciprocated. *Thank goodness!* It remained this way for the rest of my time at this location. Later, I found out he was having an affair with one of the employees. The sad thing was that everyone knew, but pretended not to know anything. This challenge with the assistant became a great advantage because I made a promise to myself to never enter into a romantic relationship with someone at my workplace.

One morning, I was asked to pick up the morning biscuits with butter from the local café. It was customary for the team to eat biscuits with butter and drink a small Coke before opening the doors for the customers. I agreed to do so and set out to the café, only a few blocks from the bank. While I was walking, I was trying to decide, *Do I go in the front door, or do I go through the back door?* In the early '70s in certain areas in the south, blacks did not go through the front door.

When I reached the café, I watched which customers entered through the front door or the back door. No blacks went through the front door, so I followed the crowd going in through the back door. I felt humiliated that I was working at the bank, assisting the same customers who were in the café, but was not permitted to go through the café's front door. I still remember the look on the faces of the ladies serving breakfast as I walked in. I gave them my order of biscuits and butter. A young woman wrapped the biscuits and placed them in a paper bag. The smell of the biscuits was awesome, and butter was oozing from the brown paper bag. The ladies smiled as they continued their whispering conversation. I am sure they saw my uncomfortable body language. I wondered, *What were they saying? Were they laughing? Did they feel sad for me?* I paid for the biscuits, thanked the ladies with a smile, and quickly exited. As I walked back to the bank, I promised myself never to go back to that café until I was welcomed into the front door.

When I arrived at the bank, I told Ms. Bella I was not going back to the café for any reason. I told her having blacks only go through the back door was not right and that the restaurant should be open to everyone. She listened and said she understood why I felt this way, but changing traditions would take time. I struggled with the word "time." How long would it take to change something so simple?

It took years before the restaurant allowed blacks to enter through the front door and even when it was allowed, many black customers still felt uncomfortable going through the front door. That visit to the café reminded me of everything I had been through in my childhood. Today, I will never go to a restaurant and sit in the back. It brings back too many memories. Whether it's riding on a bus, going to church, or any other event, FRONT ONLY.

Chapter 5

The Wedding

In high school, I fell in love with Wayne, a young man who had the most wonderful family. His mother and father exhibited their love and respect for each other publicly and focused their lives on the family. I met Wayne at a family member's funeral. Back in the '70s, it was customary to meet your future spouse at a church, funeral, or a family gathering. It was said that our grandmothers got together when we were babies and decided that one day we would meet and possibly get married.

I felt a connection the first time I met Wayne. We stood outside the funeral home and talked for hours. When our parents said it was time to head home, we agreed that we would stay connected, whether through writing or the telephone. He was perfect, and I knew my parents would love him because they were familiar with his family. As we say in Louisiana, "They are good people." It was not long after we met that he was regularly visiting my parents' home. We would sit in the parlor or eat lunch or dinner with the family. My family quickly developed brother and son relationships with him. In the '70s, we did not date; we sat in the parlor with the door open so our parents could monitor us. Today I laugh when I think about us sitting in the parlor.

Wayne was a restless individual, unsure whether he should continue the family tradition of owning a business, go to college, or follow another family tradition of joining the armed forces. We would sit for hours talking about his short- and long-term plans. Looking back, we did not talk about my plans. I should have picked up on the one-sided conversations, but I was young and had no experience in the world. All I knew was I wanted this relationship to work, no matter what. As he struggled with his future, he continued to work in the family-owned business. I loved going over to his family's home. He had three younger sisters who were a joy to be around, always hosting house parties, family meals, or other fun activities.

One Sunday afternoon, he arrived as he had done so many times before. Everyone greeted him with a hug and, like a good, guest-ready Louisiana family, asked him what he would like to eat. Once we were alone in the parlor, Wayne shared with me that he had made his decision; he was going into the military. He explained that he had a great desire to travel the world. I sat there feeling this was the end of our relationship but was too afraid to share my feelings with him. That night, I cried myself to sleep, wondering where this would take us.

His family was sad that he was leaving the family business but happy he had decided to move forward with his life. The week before he left for boot camp, his family threw a party for him. Lots of family and friends attended. While it was a joyous event, family members became upset about him possibly being deployed to defend our country. Many cried uncontrollably, but he held strong because he knew it was the right decision at the time.

Wayne was to travel by bus to the military training camp. Mom, Dad, his three sisters, and I drove him to the Greyhound bus station. It was a beautiful night: the sky was clear, and the stars were shining brightly. It did not take long for the bus to arrive. We hugged goodbye, knowing this was just for a short time. We all stood together holding hands as we watched the bus drive off into the night.

To help the family through the coming months, every weekend I would travel to his parents' house and spend time with them. During these many visits, I truly got to know the family. They soon became my second family. Everyone took care of each other and ensured that conversations helped each other through the difficult days. We also spent hours writing letters and preparing packages for the many servicemen at training camp.

Soon after Wayne returned from training camp, he proposed to me, privately, at his parents' home. He also informed me he would be stationed overseas. I was thrilled with the proposal of marriage, and I agreed to wait for his return. It's what every young girl in the '70s seemed to dream of: marriage, a home, and one day, children. Also, my grandmother's prediction was coming to fruition. His tour overseas was for a short time, but we would be together for a lifetime. Soon after the proposal, we said our goodbyes and agreed to write or call often until the wedding day.

There was a wedding to plan, so I started working on getting the photographer, ordering the cake, booking the reception hall, and designing the invitations. My mother was so excited to design and sew my wedding gown and bridesmaids' dresses. Lots of work needed to be done to meet the March deadline.

In January, two months before the wedding date, I received a call from Wayne telling me that the wedding was off. I asked him "why," but he had no reason. He just needed me to move on with my life.

I hung up the phone in total disbelief. *Did I just dream this conversation? What could have happened that would cause him to call off the wedding? Was it my last letter?* In tears, I quickly called his mother, but she was just as surprised. She tried her best to console me. I hung up the phone, got in my car, and drove to church. I sat in a pew alone, crying and praying, trying to understand why this had happened to me.

The next day it was hard to keep from crying at work. I shared the news with Ms. Bella who said, "Give him time, it will work out," but I knew in my heart this was final. Friday evening, I decided to go to Wayne's family home. His mother and sisters greeted me at the kitchen door in tears. They did not know what to say other than "I am sorry."

About a month later, I overheard my mother on the phone talking to a family member about the availability of my wedding gown and bridesmaid dresses. *What? Sell my gown?* I did not want to talk about it. I wanted to disappear or die. At eighteen, I felt my world was over. I had wanted to pack my bags and move away but feared my parents would disown me. Thank goodness for my job at the bank; it saved me. The job gave me a reason to wake up every morning and focus on something new every day. Today, I sometimes wonder what would have happened if I had run away. Where would I be today?

One day, I came home from work, and my mother excitedly shared she had found someone to buy the dresses. A friend of the family's daughter was getting married, and the family would be having a quick wedding. I stood in disbelief that this was happening. *Sell my wedding dress?* To make matters worse, I was asked to attend the wedding. How could I attend a wedding that was supposed to be my wedding?

Our friend's wedding date arrived faster than expected. That day, I tried to find a reason not to go. I knew supporting her was the right thing to do, so I decided to attend. As I entered the church, I felt my body go numb. It seemed everyone was looking at me. If I saw someone leaning over, I knew they were saying "poor little girl" or "you know the wedding attire today is from her canceled wedding." I slowly walked to my seat and sat down. I did not talk to anyone, but I put on my best fake smile and waved at family and friends. All I wanted to do was run, run until I could not run anymore. As the bridesmaids walked down the aisle, tears rolled down my face. I looked up and tried hard to control my tears but struggled to do so. The ceremony took forever, or it seemed that way. Right after the wedding vows, I quietly exited the church and ran to my car.

Back home, I went to our local church alone and sat in the empty pew praying and asking, "Why? Why me? Why now?" That wedding day was a dark day for me. I do not remember the details of the ceremony, but only the pain I felt.

Chapter 6

Wake Me Up

March came and went. As I still had no explanation for Wayne's sudden cancellation, it was difficult to move on, but I tried.

One day I went to the local store, and a young man working there waved at me. His acknowledgment made me uncomfortable because he was white. In the '70s, dating between races was not accepted in our small town. As the weeks continued, I returned to the store for my regular shopping. The young man, Ryan, started having conversations with me. One day, Ryan asked me out on a date. I explained to him that dating was not possible, but there was no harm in being friends. He then requested if it was okay for him to come over to my parents' home. It took many requests, but I finally said yes to him coming over for a visit. My mother was thrilled I had found a new relationship. My father, however, would not respond to any conversations about Ryan. In fact, he showed no emotion when others talked about my new friend.

Ryan started coming over on a regular basis. We talked a lot about my recent canceled wedding and the hurt I was still feeling. He listened and showed no judgment about what had happened in my previous relationship. I felt heard and accepted. We continued to see each other, whether at his job or my parents' home. About three months into the relationship, we were sitting on the steps of my parents' home, and Ryan said, "Let's get married." I heard "yes" coming out of my body, letter-by-letter: "Yeeesss." It was an automatic, non-emotional response.

Did I really say yes? What is wrong with me? Didn't you want to run away and start over in another place? Why is the word "yes" coming out of my mouth? Please, someone, wake me up from this dream!

I felt rejected by Wayne and took solace in Ryan's— anyone's—acceptance. And I somehow felt responsible for my failed wedding to Wayne, as though I'd let my family down. Maybe marrying Ryan was my chance to hold my head high again.

Ryan was excited to ask my parents for my hand in marriage. My mother was joyful with the news and quickly gave her blessing. My sisters were upset that I was marrying Ryan because they knew that I was still in love with Wayne. My father hung his head. I knew I was disappointing him. He finally looked up and said, "This will be a hard road for the both of you."

When Ryan shared the news of our upcoming wedding with his family, they were not very happy, because they knew there would be family members who would reject the idea of a mixed marriage. I am sure they were also concerned for their son's safety—not long after the announcement, white people who knew our families started threatening bodily harm if we went through with the wedding. Fear took over the conversations, and the wedding plans became a secret to family and friends. We decided we would only share the news with immediate family.

As part of our family tradition, we were expected to visit our grandparents, godparents, and other relatives to get their blessings before the wedding day. My mother and I spent the next few days visiting the close relatives on our list. When we arrived at my godmother's house, she was surprised I wanted to marry someone she did not know. She asked, "Are you sure about this decision? Do you understand the road you will travel?"

As we drove home, my mother spoke to me but I was distracted. I was thinking about my godmother's words and wondering what my mom's thoughts were about the conversation. What was she thinking? Was she afraid for her daughter? I just kept thinking, *Is this really happening? Will someone save me?* You were right, godmother, during the early '70s, a small town in Louisiana was not ready for a mixed marriage.

My mother was again in preparation mode for the wedding. Once again, she made my wedding gown and the bridesmaids' dresses. She also made all the cakes for the reception. The small reception of cake and punch was to be held at my parents' house.

A month before the wedding, we had an appointment with the priest to prepare for the August wedding. We had no classes to prepare us, just a discussion of the event's agenda, day, and time. We decided on a Friday at 3 p.m. because of the threats we had received. The priest felt a weekday wedding would be an unexpected exception to the typical Saturday wedding, helping throw-off any nefarious plans. We were only to invite close family members.

The wedding day was a beautiful afternoon. As we were getting ready to leave for the church, one of my sisters said, "Wake up, you do not love him." But I did not know how to wake up. We arrived at the church on time. As instructed by the priest, only a few family members were invited, for fear of retribution. As my father started to walk me down the aisle, I prayed Wayne would arrive and stop the wedding. I wanted to tell my father I had changed my mind, but no words came out.

The wedding ceremony was quick—not your typical church wedding. I do not remember saying my vows, only the priest announcing our names as a couple. There was no turning back. As we walked out of the church, I was thinking, *You just married someone you do not love, and you just committed to spending the rest of your life with him.* NO! It could not be. Again, I wanted to run. We got in my car and drove to my parents' home for the reception. Cake and punch were served. I kept looking at the front window hoping Wayne would arrive, but he did not.

Weeks later, my mother said Wayne was back and that he was devastated I was married. His parents had shared the news of the wedding, and he was hoping to arrive in time to stop it. Unfortunately, he had arrived one day too late.

Chapter 7

The Breakup

I woke up to a marriage that was not meant to be.
After the wedding, I transferred to the main office of the bank, located in another city. My new position was a promotion from the back-room operations to a face-to-face interaction with customers. However, since I am light-skinned, it wasn't immediately clear to many customers that I was black.

I soon learned some customers were not supportive of people of color working in the bank. They were not afraid to use the N-word in front of me when describing a person of color working or banking there. I would ask myself, *How do I serve a customer who speaks and thinks this way? How do I walk the line in my reactions, knowing this is wrong but not wanting to get fired?* I knew this type of conversation was a way a life for many. I remembered with admiration how the bank president from my previous office had shown no emotion when he met with me and my mother regarding the harassment. I decided to work on my facial expressions in the mirror. However, I could tell from others' reactions I was still not doing well in hiding my feelings.

Whenever someone found out I was black, either through my conversations with them or through a heads-up from another coworker, they apologized for "maybe" having said something inappropriate in front of me. First, they would want me to know how many black friends they had. Second, they would suddenly start inviting me to events, presumably for redemption. However, I did not want to be friends with someone who had racist views. I only wanted people to look at me for being me.

My commitment to changing how people reacted to race was not working in this environment. Every day I was on guard, waiting for someone to say something inappropriate. I spent too many hours in my head trying to establish my response. It was like standing on an iceberg about to crack any moment. To make matters worse, my husband was struggling with how people reacted to our mixed marriage.

One day we were shopping for groceries and ran into a friend of his family. The friend, apparently mistaking me for a white woman, started asking what town and family I was from. When I said my maiden name, and he realized which family I belonged to, his smile faded to a frown. Ryan quickly ended the conversation, and within minutes, we were out of the store and headed to the car. Was Ryan afraid? Or was he ashamed?

I knew our marriage was quickly diminishing. Ryan was extremely jealous of anyone who spoke to me, but I worked at the bank and talked to customers all day long. Once, when I was working in the bank drive-thru and had a long line of customers, someone in line was revving their engine. It was so loud some customers commented on it when they drove to my window. About thirty minutes later, Ryan drove up to the window and asked why I was taking so long talking to customers.

We argued about anything and everything. When I tried to confide in Ryan about what was happening at work, he became even more fearful he would be judged negatively for marrying me. With fear surrounding our lives, we did not have a social circle or any friends. We isolated ourselves in work and family. I knew I needed to get out of the marriage, but did not know how.

One morning I woke up early and started getting ready for work, but I did not feel like myself. As I was driving to work, I felt nauseated. I realized I was pregnant. When I arrived at work, I immediately sought my friend and coworker, Rachael. She was always a great support and confidante.

Rachael was busy at her desk researching some documents for a customer. When I said good morning, she knew from my freely flowing tears something was not right. I told her that if I were pregnant, I would try my best to make the marriage work. I could feel her looking into my soul. She knew that I was saying this for the benefit of the baby and not for my happiness, but she smiled and assured me she would support me no matter what I decided.

I quickly wiped my tears as my manager and other employees entered the department. I put on a happy face and went to work. A week later my suspicion was confirmed—I was pregnant. Rachael went from being a friend to a coach. We had many conversations about everyday life, marriage, culture, and anything else of interest. She was the foundation I needed to get through that challenging time.

Right after my son was born, Rachael moved to another state. We kept in touch as often as possible. One day she invited my son and me over for a visit, and I was excited to talk with my friend again. We talked about my marriage troubles and my religious beliefs concerning divorce. I had a fear that divorcing my husband would be condemned by my family and would negatively affect my son. While we were talking, Rachael abruptly stopped the conversation, looked at me and said, "You do not have to stay married." The words felt like she was giving me permission to get out of the marriage. I could feel the weight on my shoulders lift. At that moment, I decided to file for a divorce.

The following day, I told Ryan the marriage was a mistake and I was moving out. I started the divorce proceedings, which required that we live apart for six months before being granted a divorce. When we appeared in front of the judge, my soon to be ex-husband shared a story of an affair he had been having. The judge asked a few more questions and granted the divorce early. I did not know whether Ryan was truly having an affair or made up the story to avoid the six-month wait, but I did not care how or what—I just wanted out of the marriage. When the judge took his gavel and said it was final, I ran out of the courtroom. I was finally free! Free from the ugliness of our time together. The only blessing from our marriage was the birth of our son.

News travels fast. Soon after the divorce was final, I received a call from Wayne. He wanted to meet with me if I was open to doing so. I hesitantly agreed on the date and time. When I hung up the phone, I quickly walked to the bathroom. I felt nauseated and faint. *What will I say? What will he say? Will I finally get a reason for the wedding cancellation? Why did he want to see me now?*

When my son and I arrived at his parents' house, everyone was delighted to see us. It was like stepping back in time. However, the conversations with Wayne were awkward and painful. I discovered he had felt dissatisfied with his choices and success so far in life, and therefore had felt too ashamed or inadequate to marry me. Yet the reasons for the breakup were no longer important. Every time my son needed attention, I saw the look on Wayne's face. He was uncomfortable, confused and at a loss for words. I knew then that being together was not to be. It was time to move on.

When Ryan and I separated, my son and I moved into an apartment with two co-workers. God had his hand on me because there was no way I would have been able to afford childcare, rent, food, and other necessities alone. After a few months, I contacted Rachael to tell her I was

Dare to Be the Change

ready to move out-of-state. This decision would allow me to start over. Rachael was excited to hear about my plans. She set up an interview for the following week between me and the bank she was employed with. The interview went well, and they offered me the job with a substantial increase in salary. I contacted my sister to share my good news. Having just graduated from college, she decided to move to the new state with me. She later told me that she was not going to let me move to a large city alone. Thank goodness because, being a single mom, there was no way I could have afforded the cost of living without a roommate.

Our move was effortless because we had only our clothes. We quickly found an unfurnished apartment near my new job. My sister landed some job interviews. It did not take her long to find the right position. We had to work for months before we could afford furniture, and we were eating lots of Vienna sausage and tuna sandwiches to make ends meet, but I was so happy to be free. It was a venture that set us up for the great things to come.

Chapter 8

New Beginnings

It was 1978, and this new city was alive with cultures from all over the world. No one was talking about "black" or "white" or "who's your people." Instead, the conversation focused more on topics like work, family, and traffic. I loved it because I no longer felt targeted for my race.

Still the inner voices continued to tell me I was not good enough. One day a young man from Germany asked me out on a date. I said no because I did not know how he would react to my cultural background. The old memories returned, injecting fear into the present.

The bank I worked for was big—right in the middle of one of the busy intersections in the city. I worked in the collections department and was responsible for exchanging foreign currency, international wires, and other services. Working at a large institution prepares you for many challenges. It can also teach you how to stand up when things are not right.

I worked with an employee who was taking money from his cash drawer. After I had ample documentation, I told the president of the bank. He made changes immediately, and the employee was fired. I was scared to death the former employee would find out I was the one who had turned him in. I watched my back for months after the incident, even carrying a gun for protection. Unfortunately, I did not know how to fire a gun, so I worked in fear. My direct manager was upset with me for not going to him before reporting the incident to upper management. He reminded me daily of the levels of management. However the first time you are faced with a decision of this caliber, who do you trust?

After a few months of continued badgering from my boss, I realized it was time to move on. Also, I wanted to learn more functions of the banking world. Because the company did not have openings in other departments, I knew I would have to look outside the company.

One day a friend mentioned an open position in a loan department at a small community bank. She said the position would give me an opportunity to learn a new skill and possibly a future promotion. When I interviewed with the bank president and the director of loans, I knew immediately I wanted the job. The president of the bank was a family man with great morals. For example, in addition to asking the typical questions, he asked what was important to me.

When I was offered the job, I said yes without hesitation, and I was not disappointed once I started working there. My intuition about the president was right: his wife and children meant everything to him, and his family attitude spilled over into his work life. He treated everyone like they were his family member. He also had excellent coaching skills before coaching was the standard. Watching him gave me another perspective on how to treat others.

More evidence that coaching was important to the company was my immediate manager, who did it flawlessly. She taught me how to receive and accept feedback. My greatest learning for feedback was when she shared my six-month review. I admit when I first saw the review, I was angry and hurt. Before this review, no one had shared my opportunities, only my successes. The opportunity was that I "expected too much from other employees." For the first three months, I read the review daily, then weekly, and eventually only as needed. As time passed on, I began to understand the reason for the feedback. My manager cared about me as a person, and she wanted me to grow as a leader.

Today, I still have the review. The paper has yellowed, but it is a great reminder of not being afraid to give and receive feedback. The feedback also made me more resilient to criticism and judgment, giving me the strength to speak against unfair treatment of others. Later in my career, I started sharing my story of my first written review with my employees to help them see feedback as a gift. A person gifts feedback because they care and know your potential as a great leader. The new job gave me great learnings, but it would not be long before I would be moving to another city.

I had met my current husband, Byron, before I met my first husband, Ryan, without imagining I would run into Byron again years later. Our first meeting had been in high school, back in the early '70s at a cousin's house. He was there with a friend who was dating one of my cousins. My sister, a girlfriend, and I were heading to the beach that day but decided to stop by to see my cousin. I rang the doorbell, and my cousin welcomed us in. As I walked through the living room to the kitchen where the family was sitting, I greeted Byron, noting his giant afro and muscular physique, but I did not pay a lot of attention to him. He tells everyone today that when I walked in the door, he knew he would marry me one day. But we had very different lives at the time. He was going off to college, and I was in a transition period, not sure what I was going to do. We did not make a connection at our first meeting, and I did not see him again until after my divorce from Ryan.

Five years after first meeting Byron, I was attending a cousin's wedding reception when Byron walked over to my table to say hello. The last thing I wanted to see was someone from my past. I was overweight, stressed, and depressed. At first, I did not recognize him, as his huge boyhood football stature had aged to normal stature. He was kind and said how happy he was to see me again. I discounted the conversation thinking, *Who would want to talk to a divorcee with a baby?* Byron recalls I was rude to him during the encounter—well, I was not interested in having a conversation with anyone. When I look back on that day, I'm reminded that sometimes God winks at us to let us know we should open our hearts.

A year later, God winked again. One Saturday night, I decided to go dancing with some friends. At 6 p.m. my friends arrived at my apartment to pick me up. I was thankful for the opportunity to see a live band with friends. As we were driving to the location where the band was playing, I asked, "Why are we taking a detour?" My friend said we were going to pick up a friend. We arrived at a lovely manicured home. As we got out of the car, I wondered why we would be including another guest, but thought, *Oh well, it's a beautiful night for dancing.* We knocked on the door, and guess who opened it, standing in a 1970s dashiki? Byron.

He was as surprised as I was. Was it a coincidence or God? My friend explained our plans and invited him to join us. He agreed, and off we went. It was like we just had seen each other the night before. I felt like a teenager again. We arrived at the nightclub, and the band was playing some of the best '70s music. Though it was loud in the club, we found a space to have a conversation. We attempted to fit five years of information into one night. When we were dancing, I thought, *Why does this man continue to show up in my life?* I was afraid to enter another relationship, but something was different with Byron. He was not judgmental of me for being divorced or having a son. He was more interested in how I was making it on my own.

When we were ready to leave, Byron asked me whether it was okay to stay in touch. Our staying in touch turned into two years of dating. When he asked me to marry him, I knew it was right—right because he loved my son, right because he loved me, and right because he loved my family. Also, our religious beliefs were the same, and we were both mixed-race. We both had broadened perspectives on culture. I married Byron the following year in his hometown. The wedding was beautiful, with my son serving as the ring bearer. Not long after the wedding, Byron adopted my son because he wanted to ensure my son understood his commitment as a father. Today, my son is thankful Byron is his father.

Chapter 9

No Blacks Allowed

Our new life together required my son and me to move to my new husband's hometown. After being recommended by my former employer, I went to work as a loan department manager at a regional bank. When I arrived on my first day, everyone was extremely accommodating and welcoming. My reference from my former manager indicated I was a hard worker, a leader, and a team builder. There was no doubt I was determined to be successful as a leader in my new job, but it was not long before I realized I had stepped back into my earlier days of banking.

One of the secretaries who sat near my desk was friendly to all customers except for black clients. As I watched her interactions, I wondered if she knew I was black. One day a black gentleman went into the men's restroom. The secretary walked over to my desk and said, "Why do we have to let black people use our restrooms?" It was like someone took a knife and cut my heart out. *No, no. I just left my safe zone, and now I am back where I started? Why is there so much hatred toward people of color?* I responded to her with a sharp glare of disapproval and disappointment. I had years of experience speaking with my eyes and knew I would get my message across without saying a word. She quickly turned and walked back to her desk. As she walked away I wondered if she understood what was wrong with her statement. Just as I had done in my first marriage, I shared with my new husband my challenges with prejudice at work, including this incident. This time, my husband assured me that together we could overcome any issues we faced.

In the early '80s, some banks were still calculating loan payments using a calculator and posting the payments on ledger cards. I had been hired to supervise the employees of the loan department and convert the manual system to the new computer system. My first directive was to hire a loan processor. I called the local personnel agency and spoke to a young man, outlining the required qualifications of the role. When I finished, he said, "I have someone who meets the qualifications; however, the person is black, and your bank does not hire blacks."

I could not believe my ears. *Have I stepped back into the '60s? Now, what do I do? Does management not know I am a person of color because of my light skin, hair, and eyes?* I thanked the gentlemen from the personnel agency and hung up the phone.

My vision blurred as I sat at my desk debating what to do next. I mechanically went back to working, unsure of my next move. After a half hour, I finally got up and walked over to Mr. Russo—the bank president and my boss—and shared the news from the personnel agency. I also shared that it was best for me to resign since I am black.

Calmly, Mr. Russo requested I not resign. He suggested I go home and assured me he would take care of it. How was he going to take care of it? It would not change who I am or how the team felt about people of color.

When I got home, I told my husband I was not going back to the bank. He listened to me cry and scream in disbelief. He finally looked up and said, "I will support whatever you decide. Remember what you told me about your previous experiences: 'If you don't do it, who will?'" I tried my best to smile through my tears, but the feelings of hurt overwhelmed me.

The next morning, I arrived early to talk to Mr. Russo. I told myself to be open to the conversation to make the right decision. He was already in his office. He came over to my desk and asked me to step inside the chairman of the board's office. The chairman was sitting behind his neatly organized desk. He stood and shook my hand, saying, "This is not the culture of our bank. We embrace all people." Then Mr. Russo talked about his family's struggle when they came to America from Europe. He talked about how his family was not accepted but worked hard to fit into the community. I listened and thought, *Maybe Byron is right—be the voice of change.* I decided to stay with the company because of Mr. Russo's final comment: "We want you to stay because you can make a difference here."

The company had hired me based on qualifications, and a recommendation from my former boss—my race had not been part of the hiring process. I realized that although skin color had made people closed off, my willingness to turn this challenge into an advantage could help others become inclusive. After all, I had already helped improve my company's hiring practices. And the company's leader had echoed my twelve-year-old commitment to making a difference. Was this fate?

As I got to know the president, I found he was a genuine person who cared about people, no matter their race. My respect for him continues today. I have not made very many moves in banking without first consulting him. I fondly call him the "godfather" of banking because of his genuine concern for others and his great skill in understanding numbers. He can look at a business report and quickly give an assessment of the company's strengths and opportunities. Many individuals today continue to seek out his expertise.

As I walked out of the chairman's office, I could feel everyone's eyes. I sat back at my desk, called the agency back, and requested they send the qualified applicant for an interview.

Evidently, the officers of the bank had had a meeting with the employees to share what had happened because the secretary of the lending officer came over to my desk.

"If for some reason, I may have said something that could have offended you, I am sorry. I did not know you were black."

I wanted to scream. *Do you want me to wear a sign on my back? This is the '80s—are you serious? What do you want me to say, "I forgive you; it's okay?"*

I looked up and said, "It is time to treat everyone as human beings."

She said, "Let's start over, okay?"

As the months followed, she did everything to be my friend. Still it would take time for me to trust this person.

The following day, the candidate arrived for the interview. The interview went well, so I hired her and scheduled a start day for the following Monday. I was committed to working day and night to help my new hire succeed in the position—I knew management would be watching. I could not tell her anything of the previous days' conversations, so I stayed on guard for her, afraid someone would slip and offend her. I needed to focus and help her learn the new position.

It was an arduous journey for both of us. With two black women running a loan department, I knew it was critical for us to be successful. I leaned hard on her to ensure she was learning every step of the job. Once she mastered a skill, I would move her to the next one. Sometimes I believe she wanted to scream at me. I repeatedly told her we must stay five steps ahead. I read articles, researched issues, stayed late, came in early—whatever it took to get the job done.

As the weeks passed, it was no longer a novelty having a black person in the office, and the stares slowly turned into conversations. I do not know if it was the long hours I put in or the calmness of my body language, but coworkers started seeking me out for conversation. I no longer got quick glances. Now it was "Good morning," or "How was your weekend?" Despite what had happened, the team included me in all aspects of the company.

The officer who had given the personnel agency the prejudiced directive eventually left the company. I focused on ensuring we were ready to convert the loan department to the new computer system. I worked solely with my new employee until I knew she could stand on her own. I sometimes wonder what she would say today if she knew the story. Would she be angry or would she be proud she had the opportunity to make a difference in the company? We were successful in the conversion, and the management team recognized the success by giving me many opportunities to learn other areas of the company. With these opportunities, I learned how the banking world connected, which ultimately created a pathway for future promotions.

My next promotion was to regional manager of Loan Operations, a department that took loans from birth to death. We started with preparing the loan documents, then monitoring the loans, and finally processing payments until the loan was paid off. To have a person of color running the loan department was another first. So, I worked twelve to fourteen hours a day and sometimes seven days a week.

The one thing that bothered me was my limited time with my son. I missed so many things that happened in his early life. I remember one morning I was driving him to school and he said, "Mom, I will never be a banker."

"Why not?" I asked.

"Because you are always at work, and I miss you."

I did not say a word while he shared his feelings, but tears streamed down my face. A five-year-old was telling me the raw truth. I finally said, "This is not forever, but I want a better life for you." It would not be forever, but long enough to regret my time away from my son. He kept his word; he is not a banker today. The pressure of wanting to stay five steps ahead of the game kept me at work. I know it was also my fear of failure. I felt an obligation to ensure that I would not close the door for others who followed me.

When my husband and I married, we agreed I would work the hours necessary to be successful in my career. He also decided that he would turn down any promotions with his company so that he would be able to ensure that things ran smoothly at home. He always said we only needed one career person in the family. He was an amazing father. At the time, we discussed an average of ten hours a day, not twelve and fourteen hours. Sometimes I got home after 9 p.m., and everyone was already in bed. I would sit at the kitchen table and reflect on the blessings we had together. It was hard on all of us but, I knew it would pay off one day.

Chapter 10

Community Unity

While driving to work one day, my inner self felt there would be a change soon. I could not explain it but knew it was near. When I arrived at the office, my phone was ringing. It was the director of Loan Processing. She said the loan center would be consolidated and moved to the main office in another city. I listened to the plan, thinking how hard it would be to share this news with the team. Although change is inevitable, and we have to be open to it. After I hung up the phone, I set up a meeting with the team a few minutes before lunch. I planned to share the news and then take everyone to lunch.

We gathered in my office as usual, and I started by thanking each employee for their specific contributions and excellent work. Then I revealed plans for the consolidation. Surprisingly, the team took the change as an opportunity to do something different with their career. I assured them I would do everything to help them find another position whether it was inside the company or outside the company. At lunch, I spent most of our time together answering questions. The team was dedicated because they went back to work after lunch with the same energy they always had. I, however, could not sleep that night, knowing everyone needed to work to support their families.

Luckily, I did find new positions for all the staff, but then realized I did not have a position for myself. I started talking to my network of individuals within the organization and found a branch manager's job available near my current location. I interviewed for the position and was awarded the job. I was a regional leader of loans becoming a leader of a branch location.

The team spent hours ensuring all files were reviewed, monitoring schedules up to date, exception reports complete, and any other needed duties complete for the transfer of files. We started the process of boxing up the loan files to be shipped to the main office. Since we completed the task ahead of schedule, the move was rescheduled to an earlier date. It was a great feeling knowing the receiving office would not skip a beat in integrating our work into their regular day. The day of the move, everyone said their goodbyes and headed over to their new jobs.

As the new branch manager, I went into full force, listening to and assessing the team to understand their training needs. Once I mapped out a plan of development for each employee, I quickly set up outside training sessions or trained the employees myself. I wanted this team to be the best within the company. Not too long after the transfer, I was promoted to assistant vice president. What a journey! I could not believe my ears—finally, an officer of the bank. So many people sent cards and flowers congratulating me.

One card stood out for me: *Congratulations, this is a victory for me as well as you. I now feel I have an opportunity to be recognized.* It was signed by a young lady who was a person of color. As I read the card, I felt I needed to do more to help women and people of color succeed, whether it was mentoring, coaching, or shadowing. I would make it my mission to help others get promoted.

Working in the community required getting involved with the Chamber of Commerce and other non-profit organizations. The Chamber of Commerce is comprised of members who represent and are sponsored by local businesses and community organizations. These representatives work together to achieve a sound economic environment and quality of life for the entire community. I spent many hours talking to community leaders, seeking an understanding of the organizations in the area. I chose to represent my bank through the Chamber of Commerce because of the executive director, Ann. She was the most passionate person I had ever met. She spent hours working in the community, bringing individuals together. After joining, I started attending ribbon-cuttings and going to chamber meetings.

My relationship with Ann grew to the point that she asked me to join the Chamber's board. Again, I agreed because of my admiration for Ann's community work. My involvement would also introduce me to customers and prospects, hopefully getting additional business for my location. Once I started the board journey, I quickly became the president-elect.

While waiting for the date that would begin my presidency, I became fearful. *Wait a moment . . . Do I want to do this or do I want to back off? What will I face within the community?* I was already part of another organization that some members were not open to leadership by women.

One day, the room was overflowing with lots of guests from other organizations and the only table available was the front table. I was dressed in a white suit with a purple scarf. I sat down, and a gentleman sitting at the table asked me, "How are you heifers doing today?"

I could not believe my ears. Women were being called cows. I tried my best to ignore him. The other individuals at the table looked away in silence. Not answering only made him continue the conversation. He looked again at me and said: "Why are you dressed like the blessed Virgin Mary"?

I knew then I should have listened to the other members' warning. I continued to ignore him throughout the meeting. I knew this would be the same table to oppose a woman or a person of color as president of the Chamber.

The week the president-elect was to be announced, I scheduled a trip to Louisiana to see my father. I shared my dilemma of whether or not I should continue my journey of becoming president of the Chamber of Commerce. Of course, my father said, "If you don't do it, who will?" I did not want to hear this, but I knew he was right. I just needed the encouragement and wisdom of my father.

So, I continued my journey, and the following year, I became the first woman and the first person of color to become the president of the Chamber. My first action item was to give a speech at the annual Chamber banquet. I was going to have to stand in front of the Chamber members and guests and deliver the message of our vision for the new year. I had never given a speech in front of a large crowd. Prior to this event, my largest group was a few employees, and this event was slated for hundreds. I spent hours preparing for this night. Being resourceful, I contacted my bank's speechwriter and requested assistance with my Chamber speech and theme. After lots of conversations, we finally settled on a message of "unity."

The big day finally came. Employees shared their excitement about the history-making event. Having the first woman and person of color as president gave them hope of more possibilities for the future. That morning, my massage-therapist friend spent an hour removing knots in my back. She also prayed for me to find the strength to deliver the message.

I arrived at the event center to see the room filling up fast. As I scanned the room, I saw lots of familiar faces from different organizations throughout the room. I even noticed bank employees from the home office and adjoining cities who had made the four-hour trip to hear me speak. The room was loud with conversations and laughter. I was fighting my internal demons. Is the community ready for this change? Will they oppose the decision? I breathed deeply to settle my internal conflict, but it was tough.

The outgoing president started the program by welcoming everyone. He talked about all the great things accomplished during the prior year. He also talked about challenges facing the coming year, and then he acknowledged my taking the reins. In slow motion, I stood to deliver my speech. I knew my speech, word for word, because I had practiced for weeks. I told myself, *I can do this!* I stood at the podium and looked out at the crowd, and someone pointed at me saying, "Who is she? We have a woman as president? When did this happen?"

Suddenly, I could not remember my speech. I looked over to my husband, and he smiled and mouthed, "You got this." But I did not—I could not remember one word. I looked to my left and saw a local preacher who had given me insight into what I would face from the community. He smiled and whispered something, but I could not read his lips.

Somehow, straight from the heart, I talked to the audience. I acknowledged numerous individuals by name from the different organizations, especially the individuals who I knew would struggle with the change. I spoke about what we could accomplish together as a community. I could see heads acknowledging the message needed to be said, but had not been said before. To this day, I do not know where the words came from, but maybe I had touched someone's heart because I received a standing ovation from the crowd.

After the program and awards were delivered, I sat in my chair trying my best to breathe. I stood to acknowledge many who came over to the stage to thank me for the speech or congratulate me. Oh, how I was happy that night was over! I hoped that would be the worst of it, and that people would come together. Could this start a process of change?

During my year as president of the Chamber, I tried different ways to bring the community together, including getting my company to pay for diversity training. The diversity training helped many individuals share their stories. Many were surprised to discover that their stories shared many similarities, that we are just people, no matter the race. Racism is an embedded learning—it takes constant new learnings to help one overcome years of negativity brought on by fear. Nevertheless, the training made some impact. The greatest outcome of the training was that people were talking less *at* each other and more *to* each other.

Chapter 11

Who Do You Choose?

I continued to work with the Chamber and other organizations, and build my network. My next move was yet another challenge but gave me a lifetime of learnings. Some say you do not leave a company; you leave your boss. Well, I quit my next job at a large corporate bank because of my boss's views on race.

I remember the first time my boss and I discussed race. We were riding together to a company meeting. The discussion started with an incident covered in the local news, involving a person of color and a white individual. He said, "You know, I have always had a problem with black people because I had trouble with them in high school."

What? I said to myself, *Please, I do not want to have this conversation with my boss.*

As a person of color, one quality I am most proud of has been my ability to listen objectively, even to a racist perspective. However, hearing it from my boss, it was hard to stay objective because his views could directly affect my livelihood.

My boss continued, telling the story of how his high school fight did not go well. He had taken a beating from a black schoolmate. When he finished his story, I said we must remember there is good and bad in all people. Then I asked why he still felt fear about it today. He said he could not answer why, but the high school incident continued to haunt him. Previous to this conversation, I had observed he treated people of color differently, choosing whites over blacks for projects, for example, and now this conversation was helping me understand why.

When we finally arrived at the meeting, I struggled to stay engaged. As soon as the meeting was over, I requested a meeting with my manager's boss. He listened to my concerns, but then appealed to me to try to make the relationship work. He said sometimes people have strong feelings about others, but since he was my boss, I would need to find a way to make it work. I was shocked—I respected my manager's boss because we had a long-time relationship from previous work interactions. I'd expected he would have a conversation with his employee to help him understand that this is 1994, and it's time to accept people as people.

The ride back home felt endless. My mind was racing, searching for the right words to say to my boss. However, no words came–only the words of his boss played over and over in my mind.

The weeks that followed did not get any better–instead, they got worse. Evidently, my boss's boss did speak to him about his conversation with me. Had he not known I was black? My interactions with me became the same as his interactions with other blacks: short in conversation, demanding in his requests, and standoffish in public settings. I called his manager and shared my observations of how he was interacting with me and others. Again, he advised me to make it work. I could not help him see that this only made it worse. The more I tried to have a conversation with my boss, the more the door closed. Even having the human resources director speak to him seemed to just exacerbate the tension. With no help in sight, I knew it was time to move on.

In 1996, I left the position that I loved and accepted a position at a small community bank. The president at this new bank offered me a job to run three departments and lead a large team. I was offered more money than I ever made in my career, a company car, and an expense account to ensure the departments would run smoothly. *Wow, the best job ever!* So I thought. I immediately knew I had made a mistake on the very first day. A team from the Equal Employment Opportunity Commission (EEOC) was on the grounds interviewing employees. It appeared there had been complaints from employees of unfair treatment by management. The management team acknowledged the investigation was happening but said it was just disgruntled past employees spreading their unhappiness onto current employees. I decided to keep an open mind and give the company a chance. After all, it was my first day.

As I started assessing the team, I continued to hear of issues within the company. I knew I could make a difference, so I kept my focus on the job at hand. I continued to gather information from all the branch personnel, attempting to understand what the needs were. The president's actions continued to concern me. On a regular basis, the president would bring in his management team, which included me, for meetings in his office. I realized from the first meeting that these were disparagement sessions. He criticized employees unfairly during meetings, calling out who had not completed an assignment or that had not met his expectations? The meetings were degrading to the individuals. I was embarrassed and horrified that someone would treat others this way. I knew I had to do something or find another job.

The next day, I called a good friend who owned a training company and shared the situation with him. My friend agreed to help me but warned it would take time to change the culture. First, I had to sell the leadership training idea to the executive team, then to the president. Once everyone was on board, I scheduled a meeting with my friend and the president. His meeting with the president was less than thirty minutes.

Based on the meeting, my friend suggested training the team on understanding behaviors. We were to use a non-judgmental tool to help the team discuss each other's behavioral differences, find new ways to respond to conflict, and improve the team's working relationships. We would teach four personality types: direct, inspiring, reliable, and meticulous. My friend would deliver the first training, and then I would deliver the remaining sessions.

On the day of the training, the president did not stay through the entire training session but did attend the opening comments. The initial training was a breakthrough for many. It was the first time they saw each other through personality differences rather than actions. One employee commented to another, "So, it might be important to you to win a contest, while I would be concerned about the risk associated with winning." The dialogue between the two helped clarify their different responses to winning. After the initial training, I kept personality types in the forefront of every conversation with the employees. I knew the training helped each employee understand their own personality types and improve their interactions with customers. Employees embraced the training with a positive attitude, but I sat there wondering how I would inspire a change in the culture. I continued the journey of training the team, knowing that the president was not actively supportive of the process.

My deep involvement with the Chamber continued, which entailed writing monthly messages for the newsletter, attending ribbon cuttings, holding meetings with different committees, and more. I wasn't aware at the time how much my community involvement and change-agent mentality threatened the president's sense of authority and control.

One day I was called to the president's office. When I sat down, he wanted information about my assistant, Leslie. I described her as the hardest-working person I had ever known. I thanked him for giving me the opportunity to work with her. He stopped me and said, "I do not want to see her anymore. She needs to lose some weight."

What?

I then knew why the EEOC was living here. It was true: we were not supporting the team members; we were tearing them down. I knew I could not argue— there was no winning with this individual. The best option was to get out as quickly as possible. I stood and said, "I will take care of it."

When I arrived back in my office, I asked my assistant to take the rest of the day off. She wanted to know why. I just continued to tell her it was best for her to leave. Of course, I did not know what to say to her. We were working for a person who was focused on himself and not the employees. Was it because she had spoken to him in the elevator or lobby? Perhaps she was to be seen but not heard.

Later that day, Leslie and I spoke by phone and decided we would avoid the elevator, to stay as far away from the president as possible. We both needed to find another job, talk to the EEOC, or find a way to make a cultural change. The next morning, the stairs became our best friend. If we happened to cross paths with the president, we would quickly go the opposite direction.

A few days later, I was driving home recalling the day's activities when I realized I was almost home, much earlier than I expected. *Wait a moment; I do not remember my drive on the freeway or my exit to my street.* My heart was beating fast, my chest was heavy, and I felt lightheaded. I realized something was wrong and went straight to the emergency room.

When I arrived, the receptionist greeted me with a smile, and I explained how I was feeling. Eventually, a doctor examined me, asked a few questions, and ordered his assistant to run some tests. Within thirty minutes, my husband and son arrived. The look on my husband's face said it all: *the job*. After reviewing the test results, the doctor determined my blood pressure was high and, based on the chest pains, he would need to place nitroglycerin under my tongue. I had always forced myself to handle anything, but my vulnerable condition affirmed my human limits. As the doctor asked more questions about my daily life, pressure from my job kept coming up. He warned me to make a change or find myself in an "unnecessary" position because of stress. We silently left the emergency room but had lots of conversation on the way home about my health. I knew it was time to make a change.

At work, the board hired a new vice president, Bob. Bob had previously worked for a large corporate bank, and when I met him, I knew he had great skills and experience that would help the company. His knowledge of the world was fascinating, and his ability to learn quickly was something out of a storybook. He was friendly and embracing of all people he met. Our conversations were always in-depth, interesting, and educational for me. What I did not know was that the president was watching and did not like that the employees were accepting of Bob. I soon found out what this would mean to my career.

I should have known something was wrong by my interactions with the president. I was responsible for the day-to-day operations of the retail branches, but when we started the meetings for the grand opening celebration for a new branch, the president dismissed my ideas in the meeting and delegated my duties to someone else who reported to me. I was not surprised by that move because many times he had pitted employees against each other. This was a tremendous responsibility, and he had left me on the sidelines. When I talked to my peers, they said, "that's just him," or, "be careful." I shared my concerns with my assistant and prepared her for what might happen shortly. I needed to find a new job before I would be fired.

The more I communicated with Bob, the more challenging my conversations with the president became. Then one of my peers notified me that I no longer had authority to order supplies and would have to go to her with my list for approval. *Why didn't the president have this conversation directly with me?* The supply woman said, "Be careful." I was walking on eggshells—it was time to move on.

About a week later, I received a call from the president's assistant, requesting that I meet with the president. I walked in his office, and all the other executive management team members were sitting around the room, some on the couch, some in chairs. One of the officers asked me to have a seat next to him. The president was on the phone with his back to us but soon ended the call.

When he turned around and looked at me, he smiled and said, "We are going to have a conversation about who you support at this bank. I have talked to everyone else on my management team, and they all support me. My question to you is: do you support me, or do you support Bob?"

There would not be a winning answer no matter who I chose. So I said, "I will not choose, because I came here to make a difference for the company."

When I said this, the president went ballistic. He started shouting, "You work for *me*! *I* hired you, not Bob!"

I was thinking, *Oh no, this person is not going to yell at me about who I will support. Both of them work here, so I support both. This is not a voting booth or a contest, but a place of employment.*

"I hired you because I was pressured! Because you're . . . a *minority*!"

Do I stay and attempt to continue the journey of making a difference, or do I run out of the room?

"You think you can just walk in here, and change *my* bank? You don't know anything!"

Finally, I stood and said, "If you continue to talk to me in this way, I will leave now."

The president continued screaming, so I started to stand up, but the officer on my right put his hand on my shoulder and said, "NO. You will sit down and listen to what he has to say."

I sat back down. *Am I in a nightmare? I must get out of the room, now!*

I watched the president point his finger at me and continue yelling. I waited and waited until I saw that everyone was calming down, looking down at their notepads. When I saw the president reach for his coffee cup, I grabbed my purse, and ran out of the room.

I quickly got to the car and drove home. I called my husband at work. "I just walked off the job! My reputation is now destroyed." I was crying. "No one will want to hire me ever again." My husband took off early from work and arrived soon after to calm me down. I just could not believe this had happened. I knew I could not go back, because it was not just individuals I faced, but a pervading culture. I contacted my friend who had originally convinced me to work for this bank, and told him Byron and I were coming to his home that evening.

He and his wife greeted us, and in tears, I explained what took place. He tried to console me, but my mind was made up: *I will not return to that company.* I tried to make a difference but failed. My friend reminded me of all my accomplishments in the short time I was there, but it could not change what had happened. I gave him my keys and other bank belongings and told him not to worry about me.

My assistant, the one who had managed to avoid interacting with the president by taking the stairs, resigned the same day and packed both of our desks. She knew it was best for her to move on. The experience made both of us stronger. She is a person who understands that change starts with you first. Today, I consider her one of my best friends, not just because of what happened, but because of the friendship we formed working together.

One of the owners of the bank called that evening, requesting I consider returning to the company. I told the owner it wasn't just the president, but the culture of the bank. I also knew the bank had taken a toll on my health. My blood pressure was not stable, and the medication was not working well. I had been working holistically to get better, but the doctors felt more anti-hypertension medication was necessary. The owner thanked me for my time with the bank and kept the door open in case I decide to return.

The next day, I prayed at church to clear my mind. *What had I done? Should I have handled this differently?* I had walked off the job. I sat in the church crying my eyes out. The priest came and asked what happened. He assumed someone died. I said, "I walked off my job." He laughed, said, "Oh, you will be fine," and walked away. I thought, *Are you serious? I just destroyed my career.* What I needed was someone to listen and understand what I had been through. This was my identity: a banker. Who was I now? What would I stand for?

The next few weeks were tough. Employees were calling and asking questions. They were upset I was not returning. I wanted to assure them things would get better, but I knew this would happen only if changes were made to the leadership team. Within weeks, the president was asked to leave.

While I brushed up my resume, I feared I would not be able to get another banking job in the community. However, God always has another plan.

Chapter 12

Home Again!

Relationships within the Chamber helped me find my next job. It was as an office manager for a surveying company. It was not banking, but it was a new adventure. The marine engineers surveyed ship cargo. Did I know anything about the business? Absolutely not, but I knew I could help them organize the business by finding ways to improve their office processes. I worked with them for more than a year and helped the company achieve numerous milestones. The owner of the business was an awesome boss and treated women as equal to men. He was a gentleman—he cared about employees as people and was open to them learning new skills. My input was valued, and my ideas were heard. Thank goodness he came to my assistance when I needed it the most. My walking off the job did not concern him. It was fun working there, but how I missed banking!

I was having lunch one day with my mentor, the "godfather" of banking, who at the time was at a small community bank. In the conversation, he asked, "Are you ready to get back into banking?" I wanted to, but who was going to hire me in banking? I had the reputation of walking off the job. Yet my mentor said, "Come work with me and do what you do best: develop others." Although it was hard to tell my boss and friend at the survey company that I was leaving, he knew it was a matter of time before I would go back to banking. He wished me well and offered assistance if needed in the future. Today, I continue to consider him one of my best friends.

My mentor hired me to run the retail branches and perform numerous other duties. I was home again!

Working in a community bank, I learned to do whatever it took to run the business successfully, whether it was training the staff, preparing reports, or anything else. Surprisingly, the team was supportive of my re-entry into banking. I loved getting up every morning, knowing I had a new challenge.

About a month into the job, I received a call from another regional bank requesting I interview with them. They heard I was back in the business. While I was flattered, I would not do that to my mentor. I had just started working for him. The personnel director requested I give her a call if I changed my mind. She continued to call me on a regular basis just to check in. While I appreciated the calls, I was thankful for my current opportunity back in banking. I was learning a lot from my mentor. He ensured his management team read lots of articles to stay current with business changes, and we were coached on a regular basis.

After my one-year anniversary, I knew it was time to move on. I had completed my list of goals and felt reenergized to move forward in my career. It was not long before the periodic check-in call came again, this time inviting me to interview for an open district manager position. I agreed to interview and was hired soon after. It took a lot of energy to face my mentor and tell him of my decision to take the opportunity. Just like my previous boss, he was very supportive. He felt this was the right move to grow my career.

Working for a regional bank was very easy for me. I knew my many years working for a small community bank and a large corporate bank had prepared me for this new step. The community bank was small enough to give me insight into all aspects of banking while the large corporate bank gave ample responsibility within specific departments. This was perfect experience to excel in the intermediate setting of a regional bank. The home office was located in my home state, which helped me communicate with the management team because it reflected the culture in which I grew up.

The company had just completed a computer-system conversion, and employees were not happy with the new system. In many instances, employees had to triple the paperwork to get things through the new system. Change is difficult because it's a re-learning process, and every personality type reacts differently. Some want predictable rules, while others want the freedom to make their own choices. Some value the previous relationships while others want logic or the big picture. Being aware of people's personality types, I had the opportunity to communicate in a way that would help people overcome their fears. I knew that with my experience, I could move the team forward.

When I called my new peers throughout the company to get help in understanding the new systems, they did not hesitate to lend a helping hand. I spent a couple of weeks traveling to peer locations and getting up to speed. I was in heaven, I knew that banking was my calling, and I could help the team overcome this challenge. Based on all of my training and years of experience, this was the job for me.

Back at the office, many were frustrated, including my new manager. One day during our one-on-one meeting, he listed all the problems with the system. I looked at him and said, "For us to move this company forward, we must start with ourselves." I do not know if it hit a nerve, but the next day a new voice was born. In our morning meeting, he told employees we have to see ourselves as the solution, not the problem. No longer were we going to talk about our past; it would be our knowledge that would help the company succeed. Wow! The employees' facial expressions showed they embraced every word. His comments helped them realize that they were an asset to make the company better.

We started training everyone to improve customer service consistency, which gave customers the same experience at all locations. Employees loved this because it standardized processes and answered many questions. We also put processes in place that improved the way we did things beyond the company manual. While this sounds simple, sometimes managers didn't allow employees to express their ideas. I was not that type of manager. I wanted everyone to work together.

About six months later, the president requested the departments establish better working relationship with other departments. He felt my team had more opportunities to refer business. I agreed because we serviced a large number of customers daily. Tracking the referrals, discussing the right referrals, and coaching on what to look for was easy. The opportunity to educate our customers on additional products was a win-win for everyone: the other departments benefitted from our referrals, and cross-training my department provided a gateway to internal promotions.

One thing I struggled with was an uncomfortable conversation with one of the department leaders, Mary. She asked me why I did not tell people who I am. In other words, in my introduction, why don't I tell people that I am African American. *Are you serious?* I had made a name for myself by working hard and streamlining processes, but she was concerned that I did not tell people my race. Her reason was that when people found out I am African American, they might be embarrassed if they had previously said something awkward.

I asked her, "Do you want me to wear something on my back, telling people my race?"

She said, "No, but in the conversation, give them a heads-up."

I pushed back. "That is unnecessary. When you meet someone, your opinion of them should be based on the character of the person, not the race of the person." I implored the powers that be, *Please do not let this person one day become my boss.*

During my time with her, I tried my best to offer insight to help her grow as a person. When she made negative comments, I redirected the conversation to help her see another view. Our working relationship was strained throughout the remainder of our career together. When we talked, I was always on edge, preparing my response to her comments.

Recently, I had lunch with a close friend of Mary. In the conversation, he shared with me that Mary had said I was a close friend of hers, and that she had a deep respect for me. I did not know how to respond, so I smiled, knowing I had made a difference.

Chapter 13

A New Boss, Again

Three years later, in 2003, the company decided to expand its footprint into other states. My manager felt this was a great opportunity for me to lead the retail branches' growth. This would require me to travel twice a week to my new office located approximately three hours away. After conversations with my best friend and husband, Byron, we agreed I would take the challenge.

My first task was hiring staff in an area that was not familiar with our company. I would also continue to manage my current locations. I was fortunate because my current team was self-sufficient, requiring minimum supervision. When I started the interview process, it took longer than usual to find candidates who had business development acumen, customer service skills, and management skills. This person would have to develop the business while being away from the office but also ensure that the customers were serviced properly. The assigned recruiter spent hours with me reviewing applications. We continued to interview and interview until we found the right talent.

In June of the same year, we came upon an opportunity to buy a local competitor's bank that would expand our bank's footprint quickly. The expansion also meant I would be assigned a new boss. My new boss came from the Deep South. His charge was to lead the team through the merger by finding properties, building branches, and converting the new bank's operational systems.

My first meeting with him was quite interesting. He started by saying I was not the person he had in mind to do the job. He needed someone committed to the growth model, and he expected this person to move and live in the community. I was still driving three hours to and from the office, but I had no current plans to move. I was shocked he was bold enough to tell me I was not his choice, but I soon appreciated his candor. The more I thought of him not wanting me to be his person, the more I wanted the challenge. I also wanted to prove to my new boss that I could be as successful as the person he had in mind for the job.

When I arrived home that night, I discussed it with Byron, who fully supported my career decisions. We decided, for the second time that year, I would take the position. This time our decision would require us to live apart during the week. Living apart was new for us, so naturally, I was scared to death, but I knew our marriage was solid.

The next morning, I called my new boss and said I would relocate and commit to the new growth model. The project of building new branches and converting existing locations would take approximately three years. I immediately started looking for a place to live near the office and began packing my office to start this new journey. Not only would we be building new branches, but a digital conversion would be necessary to bring the new bank onto our system.

When we announced my move to another city, many family members thought we had lost our minds. For some, the husband could move to work away from home, but not the wife.

The night my son heard we would be purchasing a second home, he called asking me if everything was okay in our marriage. I laughed and said, "Dad and I are okay. We are just part of the new millennium." I am sure it took him a while to believe that we were okay because he called or visited me more often. On his first visit to our new home, he checked the closet to ensure his dad's clothes were there. We continue to laugh about that to this day.

Byron and I often get questions about why our marriage works. It works because we are each other's best friend. We would prefer to go on a trip with just the two of us because we enjoy each other's company. It's interesting that we have had only one argument during our entire marriage. It was about understanding and respecting each other's time during the week when work occupied the majority of the day. Once we discussed it, it no longer was an issue. Byron has been part of the banking family, as well. He has moved furniture, participated in community events and once cut the bank's lawn because the vendor was taking too long on the contract negotiations. Byron and I also had similar childhoods. Both our families were hard-working Christians with close family ties. Our marriage is truly a fifty-fifty partnership. We make decisions together, and we support each other in every endeavor.

The acquired bank's conversion brought new challenges, starting with the senior manager of the acquired bank resigning. Instead of hiring someone for a short period before conversion to lead his team of branch managers, I was asked to supervise the new team in addition to my existing responsibilities. Management wanted me to observe the branch managers and get comfortable with their processes. This required me to do two jobs. From 7:30 a.m. to 5:00 p.m., I managed the locations of the new bank branches. At 5:00 p.m., I changed my hat to manage the branches in my existing locations. I had many scheduled interviews throughout the day and evening and worked fourteen to sixteen hours a day, including weekends. I loved it! I can remember many days working until 2 a.m., going home and sleeping until 6 a.m., showering, and returning to work.

Byron and I had a set time of 9:00 p.m. to connect each day. No matter what, I would stop what I was doing or step out of a meeting to take his call. We spent time together on the weekends, sometimes only for a few hours. We made it work because we knew a couple of years was a short time commitment relative to the retirement benefits.

The conversion went well; however, the employees were not happy with the changes in the culture. For example, my first business action was challenging employees to know more about products and actively promote them. This benefited customers by allowing them to make more informed purchases and benefited the bank by increasing the cross-sell ratio. However, it required additional effort from employees.

I scheduled a visit with each branch manager individually. When I arrived at the first branch, the manager had his office door closed. My first thought was that he must be on a conference call, but I soon found that this was the model. The managers of every branch worked in their offices all day—they did not engage customers or coach employees. I was not well received when I started making changes. Our turnover rate was one I had not experienced in my entire career. We were attempting to replace staff that was leaving and hire additional staff for the new locations being built. I had a running deficit of over a hundred openings constantly for months. As soon as I would hire someone, a new opening would take its place. I could not seem to get my open positions stabilized.

The next challenge was working with the leadership team of the newly acquired bank to overcome their frustration with the cultural changes. Their head manager, responsible for the majority of the acquired departments, readily expressed his disapproval of our existing management team. Every Wednesday, the acquired team and I had a meeting to discuss what was happening in the business. The acquired management team spent the two hours talking about what they disliked about our existing team. The words were sometimes brutal, and I struggled to listen.

The first evening, I called my boss and shared what I was hearing. He said that to ensure we did not mess up the merger, I was to say nothing to the new manager, but just listen. I took lots of notes and only participated in the conversation when asked to do so.

Occasionally, while I was in my office working, employees would come in front of my door and point their finger and say, "This is the lady from the other bank." I was like an alien from another planet. The stares continued for months until the conversion was complete, but through all of this, I loved it. Banking was my world, and I was making a difference.

I finally got my current boss, who had originally wanted someone else in my role, to respect my ability. The change happened one day in a management meeting, where he decided to coach me in front of all of the team members and my employees. The whole time he was doing this, I thought, *I will never do this to an employee.* When the meeting was over, we were walking out of the meeting room together, and I ran over to close the door to talk to him. I said, "If you want me to continue to work with you, how you approach a conversation with me will have to change. If you need to discuss an issue with me, please feel free to meet with me behind closed doors." By the look on his face, I believe I totally surprised him—a woman was standing up to him. He said he did not mean anything by his comments and that he was sorry if he had upset me.

After that conversation, he was very kind to me and attempted to help me in every way possible. As noted earlier, feedback is the gift of growth. Sometimes you might think a person is not listening, but I have discovered more have listened than not. I found he was open to change, and I had the opportunity to observe the change through his actions.

Restructuring of the departments brought news of a new boss. It was Mary, the individual I had previously worked with and the person who wanted me to give everyone a heads-up on my race. In our first meeting, she said I had five minutes to cover the business, and she did not want to hear about day-to-day affairs. I struggled with the five minutes because I knew that if she were in a management meeting and asked a question to which she did not have the answer, I would get the call asking why. She did not understand I was there to make her look good. I also knew she did not embrace diversity because she frequently described individuals by their race. Our meetings became so tense I was struggling just to have a conversation with her.

A change came again when another company bought ours. We knew it would take time to implement the changes and move our company to their new culture. Sometimes God has a different plan that moves you to embrace changes quickly—the Katrina storm helped us appreciate our new company in many ways.

One day I was out of town taking an overdue vacation when I received a call from my boss. She asked if I had been listening to the news. I had not; instead, I had been getting some much-needed sleep. She asked if I would turn the television on immediately. When I turned it on, hurricane Katrina was all over the news.

After I listened to the report for a few minutes, she said a large number of customers from out of town were filling local branches beyond capacity, and the branches were having difficulty keeping up with the traffic. The customers needed assistance with their accounts or needed cash to deal with the disaster, arriving with nothing but the clothes on their backs. I told her not to worry; I would be on the next flight back.

The next morning, I arrived to see the branches filled beyond my expectations. There were customers in every chair available, some with makeshift seats, and some lined up outside our offices. The employees were handing out bottles of water and sandwiches from a local deli. People were falling on the floor crying and praising God they had found the bank. Unless you were there, it is hard to describe the events. Unfortunately, some of the media showed the negative side of the story, rather than the goodness happening in the city.

Our new company was incredible. For employees who had lost their homes, our company rented fully furnished apartments for months after the storm and set up temporary workspaces. Additionally, breakfast and lunch were served in the company's dining room. At one point, we set up a temporary branch that was centrally located and convenient to our customers. The location made it easier for customers so they would not have to travel all over the city. It was heartbreaking to hear stories from customers, but many employees had been through the storm as well and understood. We did everything to make this location a place of comfort for the customers. I could not have been prouder of the team. They worked many overtime hours to help our clients. We also hired many employees from competitors who, today, have become great assets to the company.

Within the year, I got the third announcement that I was getting a new boss. This new boss was an action person. His goal was to reduce the number of openings in the hiring of new staff. We decided to develop teams of managers to interview candidates rather than relying on only the Human Resources team. With the new interview teams, we started hiring more candidates daily, but they were not always properly qualified for a business development type of company. I knew we would continue to have staff turnover as long as we focused on quantity over quality. Thankfully, a change happened again within months.

My next new boss—my fourth in a twenty-four month period—was someone I still respect to this day. He had been with the company for years and had lots of experience in the business. He was gentle but firm, and he took care of his team in many ways. His energy was infectious, and everyone gravitated to him. He believed women should be paid equally and have equal titles. When it was time for our annual review, he worked tirelessly in defending his team's competence levels to upper management. I appreciated his willingness to share both my successes and opportunities, but what set him apart from others was how he took the time to show us how to maximize these opportunities.

The several changes in bosses did not stop my determination to make the company great. Everyone was focused on integrating the cultures of the two banks and coming together to ensure our customers were put first.

Chapter 14

My Greatest Challenge and Advantage

W hen a new president was announced, everything seemed to change overnight. The new president was a woman who had had a successful banking career at other institutions. Linda was the most amazing individual—she had a gift of speaking to large audiences while making you feel you were the only person in the room. As she brought in her management team, I saw more diversity in the executive and senior management positions than I had seen in my whole career. As well, I appreciated their views on diversity and other topics. They wanted this to be the best bank in the history of banking. I could not have been prouder to work for this company. Linda also gave people recognition for hard work. She gave employees confidence that it was no longer about one person's success, but about helping each other succeed.

At the same time, I got *another* new boss. Matt was an African American who had some of the same beliefs I had in helping others move upward in their careers. He was innovative in every way possible and pushed his team to reach beyond possibilities. He was also someone you could talk to without feeling judged based on the clothes you wore or the words you used. Finally, I can personally attest to his desire to develop his staff because I attended more development training under his leadership than under any other individual in my entire career.

It did not take us long to understand the new culture. It was one of inclusivity and openness. I felt like I had died and gone to heaven. The main campus of the company was filled with individuals from all parts of the world. I was so proud of the company I worked for that I would tell anyone and everyone who would listen to me. Customers, friends, and neighbors would look at me in disbelief. I offered five-dollar Starbucks gift cards to anyone who agreed to shop one of my branches and give me feedback. I wanted people to see this one-of-a-kind bank. In all my years, I had never experienced this type of acceptance culture. Feedback was expected from everyone. You had to give it and receive it. In some of my previous jobs, feedback normally got you fired.

Wow! I was living the impossible dream and did not want to be awakened. With Linda leading the company, we saw teams come together like never before. Banking traditionally has separate departments that do not always work together, but the message was clear: we must start collaborating. What happened next put my leadership skills to the ultimate test.

We were at a leadership meeting when one of the officers requested I have dinner with him. I wondered why because this was the first time he had asked me to meet with him privately. I said yes to the request because I needed to continue building better relationships with the leadership team. We met for dinner at an upscale restaurant. We started talking about the earlier meeting and what had been happening in our respective departments. Then he said, "Look, I am interested in becoming the next city president. If I get the opportunity, will you support me?" The city president was the face of the community for the company. This person was responsible for numerous duties, but one of the primary duties was getting employees to work together. I said I would support whoever became president.

What I did not know at the time was that my boss would be having a conversation with me in the next few weeks about my taking on the role of city president. I found this unlikely, as only white men previously presided as city president.

About two weeks later, I was busy working on a report when my manager walked into my office. I did not know he was coming to town. He asked if I had eaten lunch. In fact, I had skipped it that day, because I had deadlines to meet. He invited me to grab a quick bite. At lunch, he shared with me they had named the new city president.

I said, "Great, so who is it?" fully expecting him to say it was another man.

"The new city president is you." He grinned.

I was shocked. *Why me? A woman? A person of color?* I knew many individuals who were just as qualified for the position. He said we needed someone who understands what it takes to bring people together. I did not eat my lunch. I sat there thinking about the individuals who fully expected they would get the position. The role would be a test of my competence. I also thought about the person who currently held the title–how would he feel about this change? I told my manager I needed a couple of days to think it over.

I again scheduled a trip to talk to my father, knowing very well what he would say to me: "If you don't do it, who will?" My father was proud that my hard work had paid off and that his daughter was going to be the city president. I was another first, a woman and a person of color taking the reins.

When I returned the following day, I called my manager to accept the challenge. Knowing a lot of individuals wanted the job, my only request to my boss was to help me pull the leadership team together. The change would not be an easy undertaking. First, we were still on the journey of working together as a company. Second, the individuals who did not get the job might have felt upset that they were overlooked. After many conversations, we decided to bring in a facilitator to host a session on change management.

All forty leaders were invited to the meeting. When the meeting started, two individuals shared a list of why we did not work together as a team and why this would be a difficult task. I listened to the comments and became even more determined–determined to see this through, determined to bring the team together. As the meeting continued, everyone recounted our successes and opportunities as a community. The discussion was robust, but we struggled to agree on decisions. Unfortunately, the room was divided.

Then, Steve, one of the members of the leadership team, stood up and said he was going to support me. God must have stepped into the room at that moment. When he shared his commitment, the atmosphere in the room changed—a message of peace seemed to emanate from nearly everyone. Other individuals stood up, asking, "What can we do to help move the company in the right direction?" A few of the commitments included agreeing to work with and support each other, getting to know other leaders by having breakfast or lunch together, and mentoring top talent. Linda's vision of helping each other succeed was playing right in front of me. Steve's message became our focus: be one team. His influence gave way to our faster, new start.

The team that worked with me was one of a kind. The marketing team looked for ways to get our company recognized in the community, and the community development team helped engage employees in community activities. I had many speaking engagements, attended community events, and spent more time with clients. My assistant, Ellen, was the best person to be my working partner. She never raised her voice or got upset. She did everything in her power to make others look good.

One activity that always brought new interest was called "walk the floor." Once a quarter, we went to every department in the building and shared what had happened last quarter and what was going on in the community this quarter. Because of the "walk the floor" activity, we always recruited new and existing employees to become active in the community. Whether it was to plant flowers for a school, redesign a library, or gather food for the less fortunate, the team was there. As time continued, more employees participated. We were no longer the new bank on the block; we were a bank truly woven into our community.

My favorite project was bringing together young girls from grades nine through twelve for a day of possibilities. We brought in speakers who talked about bullying or other topics relevant to young girls. Major department stores were kind in providing clothes for a style show on how to dress. However, the networking in connecting the girls with others within the city was priceless. Sometimes when I was out and about, a young lady would come up to me and remind me of how that day made a difference in her life.

What had seemed like my greatest challenge became my greatest advantage. I was given the opportunity to bring a team of employees together to make a difference in a community. The resistance to change for some individuals was no longer the focus—change became their opportunity to impact others. Linda and Matt opened that door; they were the voice in the room.

Chapter 15

Ending Forty Years in Banking

One early morning around 5:30 a.m., my assistant, Ellen, and one of the marketing team members, Larry, were with me heading to a local television station for a routine interview about our bank's community work. As we were driving through an intersection, a vehicle slammed into the driver's side of my car. The impact caused my vehicle to flip four times, landing on the steps of a major department store. It happened so fast it seemed we were in a dream. Ellen's hot coffee went everywhere. Books, binders, folders, and paper flew above our heads.

When we landed upside down, we all checked that we were okay. The doors were jammed, but thankfully the windshield was cracked. Ellen took her shoe heel and beat the windshield until it opened. She crawled out and started the process of helping us out of the car.

Once we were out of the car, we scanned each other for injuries. We immediately called our families to let them know we were okay. I knew my husband was in his daily workout and wouldn't receive my message until later, but I couldn't help calling again and again.

I walked over to look inside the truck that hit us and saw a young girl. When I asked her if she was okay, she looked at me in a daze, and her words did not make sense. She was obviously intoxicated. She had left her place of work at a nightclub and had run a red light.

A few minutes later, a coworker of hers arrived from the club and gave her a couple of bottles of water. When the police arrived, she was questioned and asked to walk a line but was not given a breathalyzer. We were surprised when the police let her go. I knew we needed to be checked out, so when Ellen's boyfriend arrived, we headed to the emergency room. I continued to call my husband. Once he answered, I lost it. I tried to tell him what happened, but all I could do was cry. I was angry that it took him over an hour to answer the phone. Once I composed myself, he immediately left work to come be with me. We laugh about this today, because now when he works out, he carries his phone in his sock.

X-rays revealed no internal injuries. God must have had his hand on us because we walked away with only minor bruises and scratches. Ellen, Larry, and I will forever be connected because of this incident.

The accident made me reevaluate my priorities. What was God telling me? Did I need to slow down? Was I not living my purpose? I started by setting a time limit on my hours in the office. I no longer worked Sundays, and Fridays became date nights with my husband.

One year later, a new leadership team was brought into the company, and some of my coworkers and friends were transitioned out of their current positions and offered severance packages. Many excellent leaders moved on, including Linda, Matt, and others. It was a somber day because no one was ready. So many questions were unanswered. Employees were wondering, *Am I next? What happened to the dream of possibilities?* This type of disruption of a team causes low productivity, low morale, and deep fear. We took the attitude of moving forward and not dwelling on the loss of friends. I spent months in conversations trying to calm the nerves of many employees and worked hard to retain the top talent.

On Linda's final visit to the team, she said something to me I will always remember. She said, "Know when it's time to step away." I did not know these words would hold true for me so soon.

Three years later, I was hosting an annual conference for all managers within the region. The conference featured different speakers and partners who worked side by side with us. The time away from the office gave us an opportunity to reflect, celebrate our accomplishments, and strategize on our opportunities. Suddenly, my boss' assistant called to say my boss would be attending the event. I found this strange because this would be the first time my boss would be visiting my region.

When my boss arrived, she had another department director with her. They sat through each day taking notes and not engaging in a lot of conversation. At the end of day one, I called my husband and said, "Something does not feel right." They continued this behavior for the second and third day.

After the final day, my boss requested I meet with her to debrief the event. She started by saying changes were coming soon and asked whether I would be ready for them. There would be another reorganization of our line of business, and someone would be out of a job. She asked whether there was another department I was interested in and offered some suggestions. I sat dazed— after forty years in banking, it was my turn. I told her I loved what I was doing and wasn't interested in another department. I told her I would have to think about this and get back with her. We agreed we would talk in one week.

My ride home that night was tough. I started thinking of past employees who had faced this type of decision. *Yes*, I thought, *change is inevitable, and we have to be open to it.* I also thought of our previous president, Linda, and her final words to me: "Know when it's time to step away." Was this my time to step away?

I'd known many who had been transitioned over the years. When Consumer Lending was centralized, a well-respected consumer lender we had worked with for years was upset. He told everyone he was not open to a new job as a personal banker. That night, he went home and had a stroke. For weeks, he was in intensive care, and his family spent every day praying he would wake up. When he did, he could no longer speak. The stroke had damaged his vocal chords.

Another friend had a similar reaction to transition. She was transitioned out after more than thirty years in banking. In every conversation, she would retell the story of working for years and not being appreciated. Today, twenty years later, she still tells the story. I did not want to be her.

Observing those two and looking back at my car accident prepared me to live life to its fullest. I realized family was the most important element in life, and that when a transition happens, family is one's core. I vowed I would never let a job affect me the way it affected those two. I wanted to move forward without hatred or regret. I would take care of myself.

That evening I called my best friend and husband, Byron. He said, "Honey, if she really wanted you to stay, she would have talked to you about your new responsibilities rather than asking if another department interest you. Every conversation we've had lately was about fear of who will be laid off next. Can you continue to live like this?"

The next few days I walked around numb, struggling to focus. This was not a conversation I could share with anyone other than Byron. In meetings with my employees, I would tell myself, *It's show time!* Then I would get in my car at the end of the day and cry all the way back home.

The scheduled day for that follow up conversation came fast, and I still was unsure what I would say. I was hoping she would say, "We want to keep you for all the years and hard work you have done and will continue to do." But that was not to be. I decided it was best to take the severance package. She seemed relieved she did not have to choose between another employee and me. I know I made her life easier by accepting the package, but I could not continue working for someone who did not see my value.

The day before my fifty-ninth birthday, the company announced to my team of direct reports that I was leaving the company. Many cried, but I held my tears and hugged each employee. I stood strong and told them, "Do not worry about me, take care of yourself and move forward." Reassuring them made them feel better; however, I hurt like someone had cut me and I was bleeding inside. How many times had others similarly reassured me and I hadn't understood what they were going through? My identity was banking; it's all I knew. No matter what I did, I could not stop the pain.

The next day, the broader announcement was made to the entire company. The calls started coming in—so many that my husband had to answer my phone. I could not talk to anyone because each caller invariably wanted to know what had happened or was crying. I had two months to get things organized before my final day with the company. Leaving meant packing my office and completing any outstanding projects.

The next morning, I opened my inbox to find only ten emails. I normally got over 250 emails a day. Apparently, the direction from management was to cut all correspondence with me and redirect it to the new boss. While I understood this was necessary, it was like someone had cut my wrist. I could not stop the blood gushing out of my arm. My blood pressure started to rise, and I knew I needed to do something. My husband offered to call my best friend, Chris, and fly us to his home in Denver. I said yes because I could not stop crying. My best friend had spent just as many years in banking, so I knew he would understand.

Talking about the transition to someone else in banking was great. As time passed, I was shocked many close friends within the banking community did not call me. I asked someone why they thought this was happening, and she said the employees were scared to talk to me, fearing they would be next on the list. *Are you serious? This is the time you reach out and have conversations to support others.* To this day, many I considered close friends have not called.

Two months passed and the new year arrived. My inbox was cut off totally, and the phone stopped ringing, except from the few who wanted the gossip as to why I was chosen. I remember sitting on my back porch, seeing the reality in front of me. I felt like my life was over. *Is this what retirees experience when retiring? Is this why many individuals get sick and die?* I was not ready to go through the stages of denial, anger, and depression. I wanted to be a strong person and get up and move forward.

The company was kind enough to schedule an executive coach to help me rewrite my resume and freshen up my interview skills. One day, my coach asked me, "How old are you?" When I said fifty-nine, he said, "We must find you a job before you hit sixty or it will be nearly impossible to find you a job." I appreciated his candor but couldn't believe our culture did not embrace all the knowledge of someone who worked forty years in banking. I started thinking about Linda's words again, "Know when it's time to step away."

Chapter 16

Who Am I? What Do I Stand For? Why Am I Here?

I have asked these three questions of myself and others for years. Before this change, I had no problem answering the questions. Now I was sitting on the back porch going through the stages of grief. I questioned my self-worth and what to do next. Should I find another banking job or should I step out and do something different? The loss of my identity as a banker paralyzed me. I was still contemplating why this happened to me: *Did I not play the politics correctly? Did I not befriend individuals who could be the voice in the room supporting me? Did I not adjust my behavior to be less analytical and more innovative?*

Each day, I woke up in the morning, made my list of things to do, checked off the items as completed, and then, in the evening, planned the next day. After a month of doing this, the list became smaller and smaller. One day, a friend called to see how I was doing. As we talked about my new life, she gave me great unsolicited advice. She said, "Until you take your toe out of the water, you will not move forward." When I asked her to explain, she said, "You still identify as a banker. Until you stop doing so, you will not move forward."

I paused, puzzled. "Who will I be if not a banker?" It took me months to internalize the message.

I have a great partner in my husband. He reminded me I have always focused on developing people. He said, "Why not make a list of things you want to accomplish in the space of developing talent?" Taking his advice, I made a list of things I loved to do.

Coaching landed at the top of the list. I had wanted to get my certification but did not have the time while I was working. I quickly started the process of finding a reputable executive coaching program. Once I found the right company, I registered for the class and started the journey of making my first change. When I graduated, I knew I wanted to focus on performance improvement. I wanted to enhance top talents' skills so they could "dare to be the change" in their organizations.

Sometimes you have to surrender and believe that things will work out. Six months later, God sent me another blessing. I was in New York when I decided to check in on a friend, Patrick, I had worked with previously. He was now the president of a community bank, and he also had experienced being transitioned out of a job. It was a great conversation, as we shared past times. Then the unexpected happened—he offered me a consulting job. It was a project to enhance his team's skills. It was just what I needed to feel worthy. I was so happy to be able to share my knowledge with his team.

I worked with them for months. It was exciting to be back in the banking world I missed and loved. I will always be grateful for the opportunity Patrick gave me. He helped me move forward. If he had not done so, I would still be in the whirlpool trying to figure out the next step. He saved me from sinking into depression.

As I was working with Patrick, I decided to go into business for myself. The first step was understanding what my greatest value would be to future customers. I prepared a survey and shared it with individuals who knew me well. The survey results indicated inspiring and developing others were my greatest strengths. This confirmed my new direction. With the help of a few friends, I organized my business. My company, Inspire

Development, would channel my strengths from my ample experience and focus me on the future.

Where am I today? It's been two years since the transition. Life has continued at the speed of lightning. I started an exercise program, working out five days a week. For the first time, I made health a priority. I started coaching individuals who either had a desire to improve their skills or had been transitioned out of their companies. Every time I coach someone, I know I am giving back. I have begun volunteering again, something I previously loved to do.

I have also had the opportunity to spend more time with my parents, now in their eighties, something I would not have had the pleasure of doing if I were still working full time. The stories they have been sharing with my siblings and me are priceless. Reflecting on their stories makes me enrich who I am, what I stand for, and why I am here.

A friend of mine, Leslie recently shared with me that in the twenty-two years she has known me, I have worked harder than anyone she knows. She felt I was always trying hard to prove something. Was I trying to fit into a man's work-world? Did being light-skinned make me privy to how some people really see people of color, putting me on guard, fearful someone might say something negative? Maybe she was right because I never felt good enough or accepted. Now, being in business for myself, I do not need to prove anything. I just need to enjoy life and give back to others.

When I look back at my life, I am intrigued by the complex impact race had on my journey, gaining insight from the difference between how I am treated when perceived as white versus perceived as black. Because of my minority status, first as a woman, and second as a person of color, I experienced both challenges and, surprisingly, opportunities in childhood and throughout my career. Conversely, I experienced both challenges and opportunities throughout my life for my apparent *distance* from my minority status—for looking white. In either case, once a door opened, I worked hard to prove I was worthy of the opportunity. Then, my skill and dedication helped open additional doors for other women and people of color. No matter how many challenges I faced, these experiences became my greatest advantage. Being the change was the path God put me on. How do I take all the lessons learned and continue to be who I am? Only God knows what my next chapter will bring, so I have surrendered, knowing I am exactly where God wants me to be.

THE END

About the Author

Annella Metoyer is a performance improvement coach specializing in enhancing executives' leadership skills so they can dare to "be the change" in their growing organizations. With more than thirty-five years of solving complex problems and building high-performance teams in the financial industry, Annella today coaches business leaders to understand personality types and behavioral skills that create strategic results.

Annella passionately serves on the boards of numerous professional and non-profit organizations, including the National Association of Women Business Owners (NAWBO), the North Houston Advisory Board of the Greater Houston Women's Chamber of Commerce (GHWCC), and the Women's Resource of Greater Houston.

She has also served on the board of the Greater Houston Partnership and the 2011 NCAA Final Four Houston Local Organizing Committee. The Greater Houston Women's Chamber of Commerce named Annella as one of its "Breakthrough Women" of 2013. In 2012, Annella was among the honorees at the 7th Annual Top 25 Women of Houston Awards. Annella was also named as one of Houston's "50 Most Influential Women for 2011" by the readers and staff of Houston Woman magazine. As an author, Dare to be the Change was Annella's first challenge, and she anticipates many more.

Today, Annella offers a diverse range of programs and services, including performance improvement coaching, organizational behavior-based design consulting, customized workshops and seminars, and powerful keynote speeches. She is her clients' trusted advisor and assists her audiences in achieving great shifts.

To contact her, please visit her website www.inspiredevelopmentllc.com.

Made in the USA
Columbia, SC
01 March 2018